Trade Like the Little Guy

How a small trader can consistently profit in the markets!

By L.A. Little

Little, L.A., 1957-
    Trade Like the Little Guy / by L.A. Little.

Include bibliographical references and index.
        ISBN: 1-4392-2054-9
        ISBN-13: 9781439220542
        1.   Investment analysis.

Library of Congress Control Number: 2008911132

BookSurge Publishing - 7290 B. Investment Drive,
Charleston, South Carolina.

Visit Amazon.com or www.booksurge.com to order
additional copies.

To my continued love and inspiration …
Nadereh, Anaheed, and Arman

To my colleague, friend and editor,
Bernice Volinsky …
my sincere gratitude as always.

Special thanks to Anaheed Little for her
insistence on the need
and assistance in editing
the second edition.

Table of Contents

Why Trade Like the Little Guy?

Y ou should trade like a little guy. Yes you! If you trade or would like to trade and manage an account under $5,000,000, you should consider yourself a *little guy*. It will give you an advantage. A little guy shouldn't trade like a large fund manager. Trying to do that will most likely result in frustration and losses. A carpenter doesn't use a sledge hammer to pound on a nail and you shouldn't do the trading equivalent of pounding out below-average returns using large-money-management principles and techniques. It is the wrong strategy using the wrong tools!

Books regarding trading seldom put forth a method and workable strategy to profitably trade like a little guy. Trading books are typically written by *big guys* – trading insiders who have managed large multimillion dollar funds. They tell you how they made millions as a fund manager and the strategies they employed. Why should you attempt to follow the strategies of large-fund managers when you are **not** a large fund manager? You're just a *little guy* – someone like me. Someone who's trading account weighs in at $15,000, $25,000 or even $5,00,000. The strategies that big guys banter about will not work for you. Not only are they a waste of time, but they can also waste away your hard earned cash as well.

Throughout this book, I will teach you how a small trader can change his or her trading fortunes. I offer a rational assessment of what you have to work with, what you are trying to accomplish, and how to do it. I do it from the *little guy's* perspective since, after all, I am the quintessential *little guy*. The methods this book proposes are the same methods that I have personally used to become a successful trader. They are tried and true methods – methods that really do consistently make money over time for the *little guy*. Through bear, bull, and sideways markets, I have used these methods in a public forum for over six years and have published those ideas publicly through my trading site (www.tatoday.com) (Technical Analysis Today).

Although the methods and my trading have evolved over those years, the primary focus remains the same:

- Protect your capital.

- Understand and magnify your strengths, while minimizing your weaknesses.
- Use simple probabilities to act when the potential reward is in your favor, relative to the potential risk.
- Actively manage your portfolio – reducing risks whenever possible and amplifying rewards.

The methods presented are not some archaic difficult-to-understand gibberish. They are not flashy mathematical models. The most difficult math used is simple ratios, ratios that can be calculated in your head or easily placed in a spreadsheet; but they work. They work because the principals are sound; they require you to pay attention to what is happening to your trading positions, and to protect your capital. They work because they put the odds on your side! A successful trader must have a strategy that, over time:

- Puts the odds on your side for the majority of the trades you make.
- Has a higher expected return on profitable trades than on losing ones.

A trader, who determines how to achieve these principals and religiously practices them, will end up being a successful trader. This is true of all size traders, large and small, but it is particularly true for small ones. The difference is that what works for a large trader doesn't necessarily work for a small trader – as you will see. That's what Wall Street keeps a secret!

I began writing this book as a result of my trading as a *little guy*. Learning what works and what doesn't through trial and error can be an expensive endeavor. I know. I've been there. Reading books on how to successfully trade will not help you a bit if the methods they promote are not a match for your particular situation. It's the sledge hammer thing again. You need the correct tools and methods which this book addresses.

You Should Take an Interest in Trading

Despite the wealth of information and tools now available to potential traders today, the vast majority of the investing public is either unaware or uncaring with respect to managing their financial future. The data is clear; individuals believe that financial assets are a key piece of improving their financial future. Household purchases hit a near record amount of financial assets in 2003 – some $696 billion[1]. Of this $696 billion, $280 billion is in savings deposits and CDs. Securities

---

[1] Mutual Fund Fact Book, Investment Company Institute, Forty-Forth Edition, ISBN 1-878731-36-X.

purchases make up the remainder. Of that $416 billion, nearly 40% is purchased by and managed through private money managers, banks and saving associations, pension funds, bank trust departments, and life insurance companies.

Imagine that, although small investors seemingly recognize the importance of wealth accumulation via financial instruments, almost half of them do not feel competent enough to do it themselves. Why is that? With an overwhelming amount of data showing that the returns generated by vast majority of money managers are no better than the returns of the S&P 500 index, why do small investors continue to throw money at these supposed professionals?

The quality of life that you will enjoy in your golden years is dependent upon the quality time you put into managing your financial future. Trading does not have to be that complicated. As I will show, as a *little guy*, you do have some significant advantages in today's financial world. You should use those advantages to create your own sound financial future. Do not depend on someone else to do it for you. It most likely will not happen.

Who Should Read this Book?

If you are a small trader, *a little guy*, then this book is for you. This book is a self help guide on how to trade successfully. It addresses how to become a successful trader by developing and following a set of sound principals. Coveting your trading capital; only trading when the reward amply outweighs the risk; not forcing trades; categorizing your trades and recording them to analyze and improve your trading style – all are examples of sound principals. These and many more golden nuggets of trading wisdom are exemplified.

Just as importantly, this book unlike any other book available to you, considers your strengths and weakness from a unique perspective — as a small trader. Small traders share a set of strengths and are hindered by a common set of weaknesses. You will not only identify these strengths and weakness, but you will also learn how to enhance the former and minimize the latter.

As a trader, you should constantly assess the trading landscape to develop a trading bias. You typically want to trade in the direction of the prevailing trend. As such, the idea of developing a trading thesis is examined in depth, along with the concept of trading differing time frames.

This book will help you successfully trade, and learn that there is a **lot more to successful trading than just trading!** If you want to be a successful trader and you are a *little guy*, utilize the ideas presented in this book. Arrange and rearrange them, molding what works and discarding what doesn't. Take responsibility in your trading endeavors and recognize that successful traders are not born, they develop. This book will help you become that trader!

Chapter 2

What Makes a Successful Trader?

With any activity you choose to pursue, the first step in your quest should be to answer four basic questions:

1. What is the end goal?
2. Is it worth achieving?
3. How will you know you have achieved the end goal?
4. How can you best achieve that goal?

In trading, the end goal is to be a successful trader. But what exactly does becoming a successful trader mean? What is successful? What is a trader?

The remainder of this chapter summarizes the highlights of a successful trader, while the remainder of the book explains how to best achieve that objective.

Defining a Successful Trader

A trader is defined as

> Trader - A person who buys and sells in search of short-term profits[2].

It is clear from this definition that one buys and sells securities to make money. It is also clear that the time frame is defined as *short-term*. That is pretty simple and fairly straightforward, although we will need to define *short-term*. When you add the adjective *successful* to the term, the definition needs to change a bit. Since we are dealing in the context of financial instruments, adding that as part of the definition reveals the following:

> Successful Trader - A person who buys and sells financials instruments and **consistently produces above average** short-term profits.

It is clear that all traders desire to make profits and most do, at least occasionally. To consistently produce profits, however, is not what most are able to do. Add to this the difficulty of consistently producing profits as a small trader – the proverbial *little guy*.

---

[2] "trader" *Wall Street Words*. Houghton Mifflin Company. 08 Apr. 2007. <Dictionary.com http://dictionary.reference.com/browse/trader>.

To become a successful trader, we need to drill down even further and set specific measures of what it takes to be successful in the field of trading – namely positive returns, outpace inflation, capital preservation, and outperforming the average of the broad indexes of the markets you trade in.

Measuring Success as a Trader

Given the definition of a successful trader, how will you be able to determine when you are one? The definition does not provide the precise measurement of when you have become successful – it simply states that you consistently make above average short-term profits. But what is above average and what is short-term?

Short Term Returns

The time period that you choose to measure yourself is important. Choosing a period of time that is too short may lead to misleading results. Even worse, it may interfere with your ability to produce those results. If, for example, you were to measure yourself on a daily basis, you would be unable to reposition effectively or take short-term losses, which many times are necessary to make long-term profits. However, choosing a period of time that is too long will defeat the purpose of making the assessment. The definition that we should focus our measurement against is short-term *consistent* profits. This seems to suggest the merging of two time frames; one short and one longer.

I would suggest that the merging of these two time frames will lead you, as it has me, to a quarterly measurement time frame, very much like the corporations that a trader trades. Corporations measure their performance quarterly and year-over-year. If you produce above average returns year-over-year, on a longer term basis, you are a successful trader. On a short term basis, if you produce above average returns successfully quarter after quarter, you are a different breed of successful trader. Why? To answer that question, it is necessary to examine the final part of the definition – *above average returns.*

Above Average Returns

What is an above average return? Is it some constant percentage? Is it some sort of average return each year? I think not. In my opinion, above average returns are dependent on what it is you are trading.

For example, if you are trading futures contracts, the magnitude of profits and losses that are incurred are much greater than those of stocks because of the price volatility encountered on a daily basis – not to mention the leverage involved. It is far greater than what is experienced in the trading of something as seemingly mundane as U.S. Treasury Notes. They are very different beasts, and the returns in one type of trading may be a glowing success, yet an absolute failure in the other.

The above discussion strongly suggests that the definition of out-performance must be inextricably tied to what it is that you are trading. Above average can thus be defined as follows:

> Above Average Returns – The ability to outperform the average gains or losses of the primary indexes representative of the exchange you are trading.

Ideally, to determine trading success, one should equally weight the averages of the primary index for each trading exchange that you trade in and use those averages to determine your trading success or failure. In the equities markets, there are significant variations in the risks and rewards *even across stocks* that are traded. Generally speaking, small capitalization stocks are more volatile than large capitalization stocks. And even within small and large stocks, some sectors/industries have higher returns and greater losses than others at given points in time. An extreme example would be the trading you see in biotechnology stocks as compared to utilities. The latter is a well established, high dividend paying stock that does not move significantly in price compared to highly volatile biotechnology stocks where large price swings are the norm.

As an example of the volatility within stocks, take a look at the following table which shows both the individual and combined results of the DJIA (Dow Jones Industrial Average), the S&P 500 (Standard and Poor's 500), the NASDAQ (National Association of Securities Dealers Automated Quotation System), and the AMEX (American Stock Exchange) in 2002. This was the first year I personally traded publicly on the web site, TA Today (www.tatoday.com).

Table 1 - Comparative Performance Statistics for TA Today[3]

Quarter	DJIA	NAS-DAQ	S&P 500	Amex	Avg. of Index*	TA Today*
1st Qtr 2002	+3.8 %	-4.7 %	+0.0 %	+7.4 %	+1.63 %	+9.60 %
2nd Qtr 2002	-11.6 %	- 20.3 %	- 13.8%	- 2.1 %	- 11.95 %	-3.50 %
3rd Qtr 2002	-16.5 %	-14.9 %	-15.2 %	-7.8 %	-13.60 %	+9.60 %
4th Qtr 2002	+7.5 %	+8.4 %	+5.6 %	-.3 %	+5.30 %	+17.90 %
2002 Totals	-16.8 %	-31.5 %	-23.4 %	-2.8 %	-18.63 %	+32.60 %

* Cumulative gains/losses

---

[3] Note: These are un-audited returns that were displayed on the site for the year 2002.

Note the wide variations in performance from quarter-to-quarter and even within the same quarter for the various indexes. This notion of outperforming the average of the averages is not a foreign concept. In general, mutual fund managers measure their performance relative to the performance of the S&P 500 index. It makes good sense. It is a measure that you should use.

Positive Returns that Outpace Inflation

As a small trader, unlike the mutual funds who measure whether they beat the returns of the S&P 500, there is one final concept that is essential to a successful trader; you must make *positive returns* and those returns must be greater than the rate of inflation. Looking back at the losses incurred by the general market as displayed in Table 1, if you had lost less money than the average of the averages that would not have made you a successful trader. The definition states that you "are in search of profits." When we added success to the term, it implies that you in fact **do make profits**. This is not a "pie in the sky" theoretical exercise. Trading is about making money no matter what the market does. To be successful, you have to outperform the average of the averages you trade and make money!

Ruling out Trading Flukes

Producing consistent above average returns will, over time, rule out trading flukes. In the late 1990's, if you had bought just about any stock, you would have practically been guaranteed a profit. In fact, you would have had to been a rather pathetic trader to not make money during that period of time.

Assuming you made money as a trader during that time period, that particular trading success would not be an accurate representation of your trading abilities. That period represented a "once in a lifetime" bull market that was making winners out of practically anyone who purchased stocks. Using the success measures I have outlined, you would have had a harder time claiming success if you had to outperform the index averages during that period rather than just making profits.

Consider further the bear market that ensued during the 2000-2002 period. Surely the combined success measure of positive returns and limited capital drawdown would have distinguished the successful from unsuccessful traders. Even if you look at a sideways market like the 2004 market, again the success measures championed here would demarcate the good from the bad trader.

In essence, you want a measure that identifies the successful trader in both up, down, and sideways markets. If a trader is successful, as we have defined them, and if that success occurs over a period of years that encompasses up, down, and sideways markets, then that trader is not the beneficiary of a trading fluke — they are indeed a successful trader.

Chapter 3

Successful Traders are Made, Not Born

A s I said at the outset, successful traders are made, not born. Successful traders have the ability to learn the landscape that they operate in and eventually determine their advantages and disadvantages relative to all other traders they trade against. Although successful traders may share common attributes there isn't a single method or trait that demarcates a successful trader. As with most professions, there are many successful methods ... proven methods that consistently make money over time. There is no one right way to trade ... no one right answer. Instead, there are many flavors and variations. The only commonality seems to be that successful traders understand their place in the larger scheme of trading as a discipline and they use that understanding to their advantage.

To take this thought a bit further, understanding the playing field that you operate in and determining your strengths and weaknesses is a large part of the battle. The playing field that this book is concerned with is the equities markets, and in particular the more liquid markets in the U.S. as represented by the NYSE (New York Stock Exchange), the NASDAQ, and the AMEX. It could just as easily be the equity markets in Japan, Germany, or England for that matter. As long as the markets you are trading in are large and liquid, it's pretty much the same regardless of the geographical location. The equity market participants are just people, and all people remain subject to the same emotions when it comes to their money. People's emotions typically swing between the extremes of greed and fear. It's the same in Japan as in India, Istanbul or Paris – when it comes to money and the prospect of getting more (greed) or losing it (fear), people react pretty much the same.

Traders tend to come in different sizes and types. The traders in the equity markets can be classified according to their experience (amateurs to professionals), their financial backing (highly capitalized institutions to small traders with limited bankrolls) and to the time they devote to their trading activity (full-time money managers versus part-time hobbyist). As you would expect, there are advantages and disadvantages to each. Understanding which role describes you as well as the advantages and disadvantages associated with that role, is critical to your success. The remainder of this chapter explores these thoughts.

Who Are You?

If you are reading this book you almost certainly are a small trader; the *little guy*. Your bankroll is limited and it likely consists of some extra dollars you have tucked away over the years. How you trade should be, to a great degree, dependent upon the financial resources at your disposal. There is a fundamental difference, or at least there should be, between a trader who is managing hundreds of millions of dollars and one who has fifty thousand dollars; the former being like an elephant while the latter is more reminiscent of a jackrabbit. If you are the jackrabbit, what advantages and disadvantages do you have compared to the elephant?

An obvious advantage is your ability to dart in and out of positions much more quickly than the elephant. Consider the dilemma a fund manager has – the task of putting hundreds of thousand of dollars into a reasonably illiquid stock. It could take a few weeks to get in and another few weeks to get back out. The jackrabbit is in and out in a flash.

As a jackrabbit, you can easily trade stocks where only thirty or fifty thousand shares trade on an average day. An elephant wouldn't even consider doing so. As a result, you have the advantage of being able to trade in less liquid stocks where price swings are generally more pronounced.

Another important advantage directly related to a small trader's ability to dart into and out of trades is that you can easily convert to cash literally in minutes with little or no slippage[4], while the large trader doesn't have that option. If a large trader begins to endlessly dump shares of anything but the most liquid stocks, his or her action will dramatically affect the price of the stock they are liquidating. For that reason, it simply doesn't happen except in the most extreme situations.

On the flip side, there are a few disadvantages of being a *little guy*. For starters, the size and scope of staff is likely quite different. A manager of a large amount of money is much more likely to have a dedicated staff that handles a lot of the busy work that takes place in trading. Things like research (fundamental and technical) and all the back office accounting are handled by the staff. A small trader most likely has a staff of one – oneself. The *little guy* may pay for some outside advice, but it's likely to be limited as the costs cannot be justified.

---

[4] Slippage is the difference between the theoretical price you should have received and the actual price you received. Slippage can occur if you are trading a large amount of shares in a reasonably illiquid market using a market order and/or may result from the method that your broker uses to clear your orders (internal versus external clearance).

Large traders used to have a great advantage in terms of transaction costs, though that has diminished in recent years with the advent of the Internet. Being a small trader, as long as you trade with a brokerage firm with low costs and direct access to the marketplace, your costs are relatively equal. If you are paying more than a penny a share, then reconsider who executes your stock trades (visit www.tatoday.com for some broker recommendations).

Large traders may have better execution of their orders than small traders due to the size, better trading tools, and potential relationships they may have with large broker-dealer firms and market makers[5]. A small trader can pay extra for better tools and greater visibility into market depth, but unless you are a very active trader or executing large amounts of trades, it's probably not worth the money or your time to delve into that much detail.

A large trader is likely to have better connections and contacts than a small trader. As a result, they are more

---

[5] A market maker is a broker-dealer firm that accepts the risk of holding a certain number of shares of a particular security in order to facilitate trading in that security. Each market maker competes for customer order flow by displaying buy and sells quotations for a guaranteed number of shares. Once an order is received, the market maker immediately sells from their inventory or seeks an offsetting order. This process takes place in mere seconds. Market makers facilitate the efficient running of the exchange by providing guaranteed liquidity.

likely to be able to trade on information that is not publicly available at the time that they are making their trades.

TABLE 2 summarizes the advantages and disadvantages of a small trader.

Table 2 - Advantages and Disadvantage of a Small Trader		
CHARACTERISTIC	LARGE TRADER	SMALL TRADER
Entering and exiting a full sized position	Hours or days	Minutes
Trading illiquid stocks	Not able to do so	Easy to do
Moving to cash when needed	Days or weeks	Minutes to hours at most
Trading research	*Better* and more of it	Limited
Trading costs	Slightly cheaper	Slightly more expensive
Trading execution	Roughly equal	Roughly equal
Information flow	Likely to see it earlier	Likely to see it last

Given the above summary, what kind of conclusions are apparent about the small trader? What style of trading would best suite the *little guy*? How about the following?

Large traders, for the most part:

- Need to enter positions that they can stay in for longer periods of time than small traders (it takes longer for them to get in and out).
- Tend to make macro-type trades and ride positions a lot longer than a small trader. They should only trade stocks that are fairly liquid and they have to either absorb losses if the market is working against them. They can and sometimes to resort to the use of some other instruments to hedge that risk, or slowly reduce their exposure over time.
- Are more likely to trade on fundamental information since they are more likely to uncover data that others might not have, or be in a position to *hear* about information that could impact a stock's performance before most others do. Large traders have access to top management and to lots of in-house research, information that small traders simply do not have.

On the other hand, small traders are more likely to:

- Be more apt to consider purchases in smaller companies with lower liquidity and for planned shorter time frames because they have the ability to move in and out rather ubiquitously. Less liquid stocks typically have higher volatility, which can be good or bad depending on how you manage the risk.

- Consider using their cash level as an instrument to reduce risk (moving to a fairly high-cash level in times of uncertainty and risk).
- Must continually find cheap and quick ways to uncover new trading ideas. They cannot trade the news because they likely get it last.

In general, there are some very significant differences between small and large traders. To recognize the differences and tailor your plan to capitalize on your strengths and avoid your weaknesses is half the battle. A significant portion of this book explores just how to do that.

Chapter

4

Technical versus Fundamental Analysis

There are two general philosophical views on how to approach trading: fundamental and technical. Traders generally fall into one of these two mindsets although there are a few who incorporate both disciplines. Although my desire is not to dwell excessively on either of these two approaches, there are numerous examples throughout this book that make use of basic technical analysis methodologies and thus it is important that we discuss this method up front and provide the logical argument of why technical analysis is an invaluable tool in trading for the small trader.

Fundamental traders buy and sell stocks based upon the fundamental health of the company as determined through fundamental data such as financial reports, management, competition, etc. Fundamental traders typically tend to buy and hold stocks for longer periods of time than technical traders. Fundamental traders believe that the best way to determine if a company's stock is worth purchasing is a thorough study of the fundamentals of a company (its competitors, the general economic climate, and so forth).

On the other hand, technical traders tend to believe that a chart containing the price and volume action over time contains a complete picture of a stock, a stock sector, or even the general market. Technical traders tend to buy and sell positions primarily based upon the use of these charts with the implicit assumption being that the chart is a reflection of a company's fundamentals.

Although these two philosophical approaches are not mutually exclusive, most of the time they are treated in that fashion. The ideal trader is one who incorporates both methods, but that seldom happens based on time constraints, information availability, and the inherent knowledge required to make such a holistic analysis.

Choosing your Fundamental or Technical Medicine

As a small trader, your concern has to be practical, not theoretical. The question a small trader has to answer is: given the time and resource constraints, which approach is more conducive to success? To answer this question, consider not only which approach can help you, but which approach can hurt you as well. Let me explain.

Fundamental Analysis – the Large Trader's Cup of Tea

Large institutional brokers, financial firms, and even large traders are heavily geared toward the fundamental approach. They typically have access to enormous amounts of data from various industries, the companies in those industries, and analysts covering those industries and firms. If you tune in to any financially related show on television, you will soon realize that the vast majority of those who are connected with Wall Street are fundamentally inclined. Brokerage firms, investment houses, large mutual funds, and a whole slew of other financial cheerleaders all share this approach. Who can blame them, it's their business. They make money selling advice and it seems quite logical. How can anyone argue that a company's future prospects aren't based on their fundamental health?

A company's net worth would indeed seem to be directly related to their financial health, their company management, their competition, the demand for their product, the economic prospects of their market sector, and the economics of the country as a whole. On the surface, it all makes sense and most of the time this information is presented as pure fact. The problem is that we are dealing with the future and there are a whole host of assumptions that go into any and all of these fundamental measures. There are assumptions about the economy, competitors, the demand elasticity of price increases and decreases, and so forth and so on. Even if you consider the financial health of a company as reported in their income statement and balance sheet, there are many assumptions that are being made there as well. In many cases, the complexity involved in the company's income statement and balance sheets are so extensive that few can really read and interpret them.

Furthermore, it is widely known that any Chief Financial Officer (CFO) can push these numbers around a bit on a quarterly basis to present a picture of stability when there is really a sea of chasm beneath. Stop and think about it. How can a multibillion dollar company project and consistently hit targeted earnings on the button quarter after quarter, year after year? You would think that there would be more variation from quarter to quarter, more unexpected events that affect earnings. Instead, smooth earnings are reported. Seems odd doesn't it? Given the wiggle room that exists in the accepted accounting practices, it really isn't that difficult to understand, and as a result, you have to wonder about the value of these reports.

This is not to suggest that the fundamental approach has no value. The point is that the fundamental approach is as flawed as any approach that attempts to predict the future. The future is unknown and the comfort that the fundamental approach attempts to offer is a facade. Don't be fooled by it. Fundamental analysis is not nearly as concrete as it seems.

Technical analysis, on the other hand, has the same difficulties in predicting the future. The study of price, time, and volume, and the various patterns that they produce in a chart can lead you to assumptions that may or may not be correct. The notion that the analysis of recent price and volume patterns of a company's stock can lead to indisputable future price clarity is a bit of a stretch as well. Anything that involves humans and the future is fraught with uncertainty and unpredictability.

Technical analysis' single largest flaw is that ten people in a room with the same chart can produce ten different interpretations of what it means. It doesn't have the concrete feeling that the fundamental analysis does. In a way, that's good, because technical analysts tend to be savvier about using protective means to remove a trade than fundamental traders. Technical analysts seem to be better equipped than fundamentalists to admit mistakes and move on since their analysis is seemingly less concrete.

Fundamentals – The Disadvantages to a Small Trader

Fundamental events typically take time to evolve. In other words, the timing is seldom very precise. Since a small trader, by definition, is usually working with a reasonably limited capital base, timing is rather critical. This is probably the largest problem with relying solely on a fundamental approach as a small trader. It could turn out that you are quite right in your analysis but quite wrong for a long time until the fundamental events you have foreseen become reality. If you act too early on your fundamental beliefs, you may find yourself in a losing trade for a very long time. Using only a fundamental approach, you can suffer a tremendously large and debilitating drawdown[6] in your capital while you wait for your plan to solidify. This inability to *know* when you are wrong is critical to a small trader since your number one priority is to protect your capital. You cannot suffer a loss of 10% or 20%. It is much too difficult to bounce back from such a loss, if you have limited resources.

Consider the following example. Let's assume that as a fundamental trader you have studied the books of Company XYZ and have discovered they are financially sound and making money hand over fist. You have also considered the markets they sell into, and all looks promising. By analyzing their profits to earnings ratio, along with other financial ratios, you

---

[6] A drawdown occurs anytime your portfolio loses value. Note that a drawdown is computed on the highest net worth of the portfolio at any point in time where the portfolio assets are based on both closed and open positions (open positions are marked-to-market to determine their relative value).

have concluded that their present value is undervalued and, rather than selling for $10 a share, they should be selling for $13 per share. As a result, you decide to buy a number of shares, realizing that this is a slam dunk.

After buying the shares, all the fundamental factors remain the same with the exception of the financial ratios. Those ratios actually become more undervalued because the stock drops to $9 per share. As a fundamental trader, the logical deduction is that now XYZ is even more appealing than it was at $10 per share since it has depreciated 10% since you first bought it and everything remains promising. So what do you do? Do you buy more shares? What criteria do you use to decide that something is wrong? What if it drops to $7.50 per share and effectively wipes out 25% of your investment capital? What if the fundamentals haven't changed? If fundamentals are driving your investment decision, shouldn't you expect fundamentals to tell you when you are wrong? Shouldn't you just keep on buying?

Large traders in fact do just that. If the stock becomes even more undervalued, they just buy more of it because they can. They have significant resources at their disposal and what seems like an endless stream of new funds coming in monthly by way of customer contributions (pension funds, automatic withholdings for investment funds, etc.). They are not like you. They do not have limited resources. They can afford to behave differently. They can continue to make purchases at cheaper and cheaper prices, driving their average purchase cost down if the fundamental picture hasn't changed in their opinion. They have virtually unlimited resources and can afford to wait out whatever is causing the price to temporarily drop. They have the wherewithal to do so. The *little guy* does not have that luxury.

Technical Analysis – The Disadvantages to a Small Trader

Technical trading primarily concerns itself with pattern recognition. By definition, pattern recognition can only happen once a move has already begun to occur otherwise there would be no pattern. Most technical analysis techniques center upon the concept of a trend; once a trend is identified, the desire is to trade with that trend. This implies that, even if you are right about the direction of a trade, you will not be catching all of a move when it occurs. The problem with this is that unless a trend sustains itself for a reasonable duration, you will find yourself moving in and out of positions on a continual basis; the shorter the trend, the weaker your results. If the trend is too short and your entry is less than optimal, the results can end up quite negative over time.[7]

Another issue is that many technical traders are pattern traders who tend to have less conviction than fundamental traders. Where fundamental traders are at risk because they are too adamant in their beliefs, technical traders are simply too wishy-washy in theirs. This lack of conviction can easily lead to thrashing – a process where you jump from one side of a trade to another and back, losing on the way up and on the way down. A lack of conviction also scars a trader's mental makeup if he or she is trading technically and suffers a series of losing trades, much like a string of hands in the casino where the dealer hits blackjack. As a small trader, sustaining a series of failures can prove difficult to overcome. If you are unsure in your technical approach, it can be that much more taxing.

Technical Analysis Favors the Small Trader

Despite the disadvantages of a technical approach to trading, technical trading does provide a couple of

---

[7] To be fair, there are subsets of technical analysis that are not directly related to trend following, but the majority of technical analysis has trend identification as a focal point of the trading regimen.

significant advantages over fundamental trading to the *little guy.*

One critical advantage that technical analysis offers to the small trader is the ability to quickly evaluate many stocks – making decisions about whether a stock deserves greater attention in a matter of seconds if not a couple minutes. Try to do that with fundamental analysis, where a cursory look could take a few hours at best.

The second significant advantage technical analysis provides is the framework that encourages traders to consider trading as a futuristic event – where the event outcome is unknown. When you study a chart, you can identify support and resistance areas on the chart; areas where there are buyers and sellers. This framework allows you to determine the risk associated with a trade by allowing you to calculate the potential losses that may occur if you were to make the trade – *before the trade is taken.* As a small trader, protecting your capital always has to be your primary goal. If you lose your capital, you can no longer trade. Without capital, you are finished!

In its simplest terms, trading is about the future. You buy or sell some securities based on events that have yet to unfold. Future events affect the price of the security. Future events are, by necessity, unknown. In other words, there is a probability that they may or may not occur. Logically, there is a probability that the trade you make may or may not succeed, regardless of whether you use a fundamental, a technical, or a combination of both to aid in your decision making.

Given that the success or failure of a trade revolves around probabilities, the most important thing you can do as a trader is to first accept this fact. Secondly, you need a strategy that can profit in this realm of uncertainty. Technical analysis is, by its very nature, better suited to uncertainty. It is centered upon the idea of support and resistance, entry and exit points, and charting patterns; whereas, fundamental analysis is primarily centered upon determining whether a security is priced fairly.

This simple analysis suggests that technical analysis is the small trader's friend because the disadvantages associated with it are less painful than those associated with fundamental analysis. Technical analysis coerces you to accept the notion that a losing trade doesn't mean failure – it is expected since the future cannot be known. In dealing with the future, it is important to understand that you will not be infallible and that incurring losses do not make you a loser; they are a means to winning in the game of trading.

Risk Management Is Critical to both Trading Approaches

As mentioned previously, the ideal trader is probably one that encompasses both trading approaches and favors neither completely. Assuming sufficient time and resources, the use of both approaches can lead to a more reasoned rationale for making a potential trade. On the fundamental side, you ascertain the possible catalysts that affect supply and demand; while on the technical side, you time your entry and exit points more efficiently.

Regardless of the approach taken, successful traders recognize that there is an intersection to the two approaches. That intersection centers around the idea of money and risk management (see Figure 1). To consistently make money, both approaches **require** you to manage your portfolio risk to be successful. This is a very important concept and one that I spend a great deal of time on.

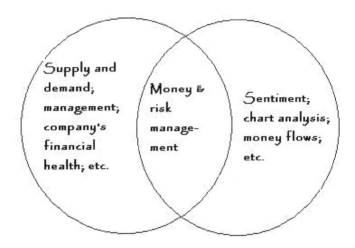

Figure 1 – Intersection of Fundamental and Technical Approach

Successful traders concentrate on the following:

- Spending an inordinate amount of time managing their portfolio and stock risk.
- Determining which possible trade is the best trade with respect to risk and reward.
- Considering what strategy to employ when entering, managing, and eventually exiting trades.

These considerations typically are what separate the successful from the unsuccessful, yet very little attention is paid to the intersection of fundamental and technical approaches. In fact, the majority of the popular press focuses almost entirely on the fundamental reasons for entering a trade. They seldom discuss how to manage a trade or when to exit it instead acting as if you never exit the trade – only enter.

As you read the remainder of this book, you will see that I utilize a technical approach in the examples throughout these pages. I also encourage the small trader to consider the use of technical analysis in their approach to trading. In the end though, risk and money management will likely define your success or lack thereof. As a trader, that is where your primary focus should lie in the quest to become a successful trader.

Chapter 5

Trade Preparation

Trade preparation refers to the methodical work required to identify trading opportunities. It is not limited to finding a stock to purchase. It begins prior to those considerations. Before you can determine *what* stock to buy, you have to first understand if *any* stock is worth purchasing. There are times when the general market and/or the market sector are tugging against the odds of making a successful trade. Even if you were to locate the *perfect* stock to purchase, if the market is in a bear market, your ability to make money on the trade is severely hampered. There is a saying on Wall Street that a rising tide lifts all boats. The same is true of a tide that is receding; all boats tend to sink lower. As a result, developing a trading thesis precedes stock evaluation and selection. Once you have developed a trading bias, then you can consider what to trade.

Establishing a Market Thesis – a Trading Bias

Many traders find themselves floundering when trying to trade, not because of their inability to pick a winning trade, but because they cannot or do not understand that half the battle is getting the timing of a trade right. Consider how many times you have purchased a stock only to see if fall soon after the purchase. How many times have you taken a loss on a trade only to check back in a couple weeks or months to see that the trade wound up being a winning trade – had you stuck around? How many times have you considered that the problem with the trade was not that it was a bad trade but that it was an unfortunate *time to make the trade*? Have you every considered that? Did you study your failed trades and perform the analysis that could lead you to that conclusion?

If the data were available, it would probably surprise you to find out that probably half, if not more, of all *losing trades* end up as losers because of **bad entry timing.** It's like swimming against the tide when you do this. To understand how to get your entry timing in synchronicity with the market, you have to look at three important concepts and integrate them into your bias formulation. They are:

1. Understanding the cyclicality of the market and be able to identify the current phase of the market.
2. Realizing that every market is comprised of the three components, (the general market, market sectors, and individual stocks) and that these components necessarily trend over time.
3. That the trend of these three components occurs over multiple time frames and may be synchronized or in conflict.

The next few paragraphs examine each of these concepts in more detail. At the conclusion of that examination, you should be able to formulate your general market bias. Having such a bias gives you a more realistic possibility of trading in synchronization with the general market. Once that is accomplished, the next step is to identify particular trades that are congruent with this bigger picture view of the market you have developed.

Cyclicality of the Markets

Stock markets are cyclical in nature. Although the concept of cyclicality is unquestioned,[8] the periodicity of that cyclicality is somewhat variable and depends on many factors. This makes the ability to predict future

_____

[8] Norman G. Fosback, Stock Market Logic, Dearborn Financial Publishing, Inc., 26th Edition, 1998, ISBN 0-79310-148-4.

cyclical events error prone. This is not to suggest that market cyclicality should be ignored; it shouldn't. It does suggest though, that being able to predictably time these cycles via some rigid mathematical precision is quite unlikely.

As a small trader, it is not necessary to identify exactly where the broad market is at any given point in time, though it is important to have a reasonably good understanding of what cycle the broad market is probably in. In other words, you don't have to know that the broad market is at the end of the accumulation phase as much as you need to know that it is likely somewhere during the accumulation phase of the market. To form a reasonably valid market thesis, you need a reasonably accurate understanding of the current market phase.

The Four Phases of Market Cyclicality

Stock market cyclicality consists of four phases[9]:

- Accumulation
- Mark up
- Distribution
- Mark down

---

[9] Blackman, Matt, Understanding Cycles – The Key to Market Timing, http://www.investopia.com/ articles/technical/04/050504.asp.

Figure 2 illustrates these.

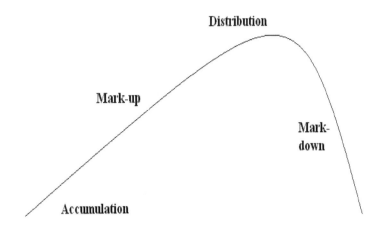

Figure 2 - Four Phases of Market Cyclicality

Accumulation Phase

The accumulation phase occurs after a substantial decline in the general price of most stocks. It begins during bad economic times when all the talk is of gloom and doom, and when a recession is generally recognized or is in full force. It occurs because corporate insiders and value investors see stocks as cheap again and thus begin to re-purchase the stocks they previously sold during the distribution phase. The accumulation phase can be likened to shopping in the local apparel store to find that prices have declined some 20, 30, or 40% from what they were at their highest point. When that happens, you figure there is some value in these prices. In fact, you figure that whatever caused this to happen is most likely closer to an end rather than the beginning. Since the valuations are very attractive, if you are willing to wait for a while, you expect that you will make money when prices eventually begin to appreciate again.

Large position players necessarily understand that to make money on their large investment portfolios, it will take time for prices to appreciate. The key to their success is to make purchases when the news is at its worst (they will necessarily be a bit early as well as a bit late in this endeavor not knowing exactly where the lowest price points are), and to slowly accumulate those large positions at an average price that is rather low. In the later phases of the market's cyclical nature, they will turn and begin to sell what they have accumulated at these lower costs. These well-heeled investors and institutions understand a value, not just because prices have decreased, but many times because they are in a position to know that the company's fortunes are likely to change for the better in the near future. These are true value investors and their superior fundamental knowledge enables them to collect those investments that are most likely to succeed when the general economy turns. These are the big guys!

As a small investor, you have to always keep your ear to the ground and look for the tell-tale signs of accumulation. Technically speaking, accumulation typically occurs on lighter volume than mark-downs (the phase that precedes it). To the untrained eye, the market may appear that it is readying itself for further selling even after having been discounted greatly already.

Another technical signal that the accumulation phase may be underway is that prices, after having trended downward for some period of time, begin to level out and form a trading range. During this period, share prices work their way back and forth within some defined range; moving from the upper part of the range to the lower price points. Prices no longer continue to make lower lows on a continual basis.

This period of time is the surrender phase for those investors who either bought at or near the top of the market. These investors are underwater on their investments and if they didn't sell during the prior to the decline, then this is probably where they begin to feel that the market will never go up again. Their pessimism grows along with the continuing drumbeat of bad news – slowly giving up and selling their shares out of disgust. The feeling that the market will never rise again (although it is no longer going down) is another palpable sign that the market is likely at or near the accumulation phase of its cycle.

Mark-Up Phase

The mark-up phase is categorized by periods of significant price appreciation in stock prices. During this phase, one sector[10] after another begins to increase in price. After rising appreciably, the sector steadies and holds generally at the higher price level while a different market sector begins to appreciate in price. The volume begins to expand during this phase of the market, which itself supports further buying. During this market phase, if you look at almost any chart, you will see the price trend for the stock clearly begins to display an upward slope - a series of higher highs and higher lows.

At this point, the negativity that was quite apparent in the accumulation phase begins to fade away and the realization that the world isn't going to end after all becomes apparent once more. There will still be bad news though, and that will keep a portion of the buyers on the sidelines, unsure if the worst is really over. This continuing bad news ends up worrying the smaller and uncertain potential buyers while the larger players continue to slowly accumulate larger and larger positions.

During this phase of the market, you may hear the term *climbing a wall of worry* used to describe the rising prices for stocks. The fact that prices rise slowly begins to encourage others to climb aboard, lest they be left behind. Anxiety of being left behind is a significant motivator during this phase of the market.

---

[10] A related group of stocks; usually in a similar industry.

Towards the end of the mark-up phase, you will hear market participants saying that *the train is leaving the station.* They use this phrase to describe the need to buy before the market gets away from you. The implication is that you have to put logic aside and simply jump on board. It is at this time that greed increases as do prices – all moving faster and faster as they continue to race higher and higher. Volume usually begins to pick up as an increasing number of investors and traders chase stocks higher. This is a time where the greatest gains are made on the upside and where the buy and hold mentality works the best.

Distribution Phase

The distribution phase is typically highlighted by greater volatility in prices *in both directions.* Price volatility is great near the end of the mark-up phase, but mostly in the direction of higher prices. During the distribution phase, price increases are slow and methodical while price drops occur *out of the blue* and with volume expansion. In this phase, the market begins to feel as if it is becoming more and more unstable and choppy. Usually you see large spike downs in prices that alarm investors, but the greed is so great that the prices quickly recover and prices escalate to even higher levels on light volume. The media is typically broadcasting that *it is somehow different this time around.* It is a "New Economy" or what use to matter no longer does; but it never is different, it really is cyclical.

During this phase, the larger players quietly begin to distribute their stock as fast as they can without creating alarm. These large sellers want to sell the majority of what they bought during the accumulation and mark-up phases to the late comers for as high a price as they can. They are helped by the greed that is rampant at this time as well as the initial public offerings that begin to burgeon.

Takeover and leveraged buyouts are typically active during this period as well. The distribution phase can last several weeks to many months as the largest holders distribute the bulk of their holdings to the latecomers. It's a delicate game, but one that is played over and over again. Technically, the most telling signs during this phase are the increased price volatility (in both directions) and the surge in prices that are no longer accompanied by surges in volume. Generally speaking, where volume surges do exist, they generally occur as prices decrease rather than increase.

Mark-Down Phase

The fourth and final phase is the mark-down phase. This is a painful period for any and all who continue to hold stock positions. It is the time where the stockholders that hang on are most likely to lose the greatest amount and end up being the stockholders who will eventually sell their stock cheaper (during the next occurrence of the accumulation phase).

Price depreciation can be quite extreme and rapid during this period as one third to three quarters of all the gains made in the preceding cycle are typically erased. The primary technical signals during this phase of the market include a further swell in volume and an increase in the extremes in traders' emotions. Volume continues to increase as prices fall. Bad news begins to be broadcast from all corners and further fuels selling as the concept that all is bad and getting worse begins to take hold.

Market Components, Trends, and Time Frames

Stock market exchanges consist of:

1. The general market itself (the market index like the S&P 500, the NASDAQ, and the Dow Jones Industrial Average)
2. A multitude of stock sectors (like technology stocks or precious metals or financial stocks)
3. All the individual stocks (companies like IBM, AT&T, etc.)

Trends, along with support and resistance, are the basic tenets to technical analysis. Within the realm of that field of study, it is a given that each of these market components are always trending. A trend can be loosely defined as continued price movement in a general direction. The trend may be up (a series of higher highs and higher lows over some defined time range), down (a series of lower lows and lower highs over some defined time range), or sideways (a series of roughly equal highs and lows over some defined time range). Note that this loose definition does not specify a certain time frame, but it does indicate that a time frame does exist.

Historically, technicians have come to accept the notion that there are generally three trends at any given time in the market – the long-term, intermediate-term, and short-term (which are commonly referred to as Primary, Secondary, and Minor by Edwards and Magee[11]). For my trading, I track four trends. They are:

- Ultra Short Term Trend – These are brief and relatively unstable trends[12] that interrupt the Short Term Trend. They can run from a few days to a couple of weeks. Ultra Short Term Trends are unstable because they reflect the general noise in the market (the up and down movement that seems so random on a short-term time frame). This trend is roughly equivalent to the Minor Trend as defined by Edwards and Magee.

---

[11] Robert D. Edwards and John Magee, <u>Technical Analysis of Stock Trends</u>, St. Lucie Press, 7th Edition, 2nd Printing, 1998, pp 16-17.

[12] There is a significant variation in the day to day prices during these brief trending periods.

- Short Term Trend – This trend is more stable trend than the Ultra Short Term Trend and the most interesting trend from a small trader's perspective. It is long enough in duration to trade in the direction of the trend, yet not so long as to have significant[13] counter-trend moves within it. This trend usually lasts from two weeks to three months.
- Intermediate Term Trend – The Intermediate Term Trend typically lasts up to six months but is fraught with one or more Short Term Trends that interrupt its progression. On the flip side, the Intermediate Term Trend typically interrupts the Long Term Trend.
- Long Term Trend – This is the more extensive up or down movements in price which usually last for a year or more and results in significant appreciation or depreciation in whatever is trending.

Although there are times when trading the Ultra Short Term Trend is both possible and advisable as a trader, typically the Short Term Trend offers the greatest promise. If you consider that both the Intermediate and Long Term Trends consists of a number of Short Term Trends strung together, you can quickly see that when trading the Short Term Trend you are effectively trading the longer term trends as well. The significant difference is that when trading the Short Term Trend, you are not subject to the larger draw downs that are

---

[13] Significant in this context would be large percentage price swings.

bound to occur in the Intermediate and Long Term Trends if you were to hold those positions over time as the trends develop.

How significant are these draw downs? For each of the trends, in most cases, prices may appreciate or depreciate as much as 61.8% of the prior move and still be a valid trend. For example, if an up trending Intermediate Term Trend is in progress and the extent of the price appreciation so far is $10 on a $20 stock, an interrupting Short Term Trend could take the price lower by as much as $6.18 without invalidating the direction and continuation of the Intermediate Term Trend. Depending on how much stock you purchase, $6.18 may represent a significant hit to your portfolio. If you were to purchase that stock right before such a corrective trend was to take place, you could end up as another statistic in a list of failed trades due to bad timing.

Let me take a moment to elucidate this thought further as it is an important one – one that is not fully appreciated by most. The success of an individual trade has as much to do with time as with any other factor. What may be a failure in one time frame could easily be a success in another. Consider the chart shown in Figure 3. You can pick almost any stock chart and find examples like this one. This just happens to be a large and widely know stock, Alcoa, which trades on the NYSE and is a component of the venerable Dow Jones Industrial Average.

Figure 3 - Alcoa and the Importance of Time Frames

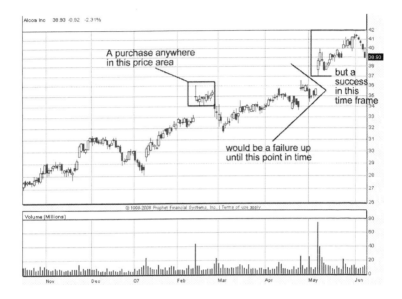

What you see in this chart is a simple concept, but one that is ignored time and time again. The *success or failure of a trade heavily depends on the time frame it is traded in.* In the Alcoa chart, if you purchased shares in Alcoa in the price range designated by the box in the middle of the chart, you would have had a failed trade unless your time frame was longer than two months. As can be seen, almost all the trades that took place after that point in time broke even or resulted in failure until the early part of May. Note that it works in reverse also, that is if you stay in a trade too long, you can end up having a winning trade turn into a losing one.

54

Time is an integral component of successful trading. Use technical or fundamental analysis all you want, but if you ignore the concept of time, your trades will fail more often than not if you are trading the wrong time frame. To trade successfully, you must ascertain what time frame you should be trading for each trade you make.

Think about it this way. We all know that the casinos in Las Vegas win over the long run. They do this because, in the time frame that they employ (which is on the order of months), the odds are in their favor. This is necessarily true since the law of large numbers implies that over a large number of samples, the average observations should approach and stay close to the expected value. In the casinos, the expected value is that the casino will win x percent of the time where x varies depending on the game, but it is always greater than 50%. Figure 4 illustrates the idea.

Figure 4 – Time, Trade Success, and Risk

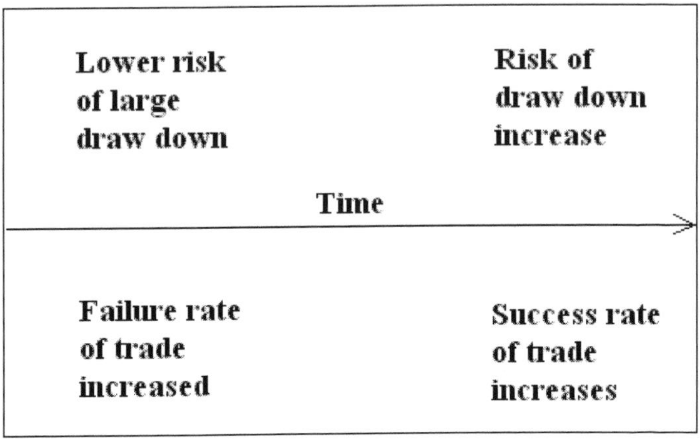

Lower risk of large draw down	Risk of draw down increase
Time ⟶	
Failure rate of trade increased	Success rate of trade increases

The casino recognizes that the longer they are exposed to players who play their games, the higher the odds that one or more of those players will strike it rich. The parallel for the large trader is the basically the same. The large trader knows that the longer they are exposed to a given trade, the larger the risk that something will occur causing them to suffer a large drawdown on their capital. Both the casino and the large trader are willing to take this risk though. They both are sufficiently capitalized such that they can withstand the hit when it finally occurs.

The small trader, on the other hand, is not capitalized well enough to withstand such a drawdown. Their alternative is to trade on a shorter time frame where the risk of a large drawdown is very small. This necessarily increases the rate of trade failures though. This is the trade off. It is true of each and every trade you make (whether you recognize it or not).

Looking at this diagram (Figure 4), it is clear that the shorter the time frame, the lower the risk of losing a significant portion of your capital. On the other hand, the longer the time frame, the higher the risk. Although this is common sense, it is an important concept and it is something you should consider when you enter a trade. If you intend to make a long-term trade, take measures to keep the overall risk to your portfolio within reasonable parameters. Although I will talk about this at length in Chapter 9, there are ways to mitigate these risks such as trading smaller on longer term trades and/or to trade multiple time frames.

Time Frames and Trends

The notion of time frames is a critical one and unfortunately is not as simple as it may appear. As a quick refresher, consider the market components of the general market, sector, and stock. First, focus on just the general market component. This component has its own time frame – a time frame that consists of trends that are somewhat independent of the various sectors and individual stocks. If you consider only the Short,

Intermediate, and Long Term Trends[14], a visualization of those trends at some particular point in time might look something like what is shown below in Figure 5.

Figure 5 – General Market Price Trend Cube

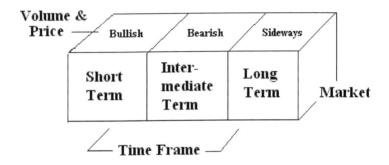

In this hypothetical depiction of the general market trend, the Short Term Trend is bullish, the Intermediate Term Trend is bearish, and the Long Term Trend is sideways. How you decide this is by examining a chart of the instrument you are interested in (the general market in this example) to see if there are a series of higher highs and higher lows (bullish) or lower lows and lower highs (bearish) or a market that just meanders around in a sideways fashion (sideways).

---

[14] Unless you are trading the Ultra Short Term Trend, it can be safely ignored as it consists mostly of random price action and its relative instability lends little to the analysis I am about to employ here.

General Market Trend

The example depicted in Figure 5 shows that the general market is confused. No clear trend exists because each time frame is opposed to the other. Why is it important to determine the general market trend when you just want to trade this or that stock? You do this because the general trend of the overall market **influences** the general trend of individual stocks.

It's only logical. If the market is reflecting rising prices in general, a purchase of one of those stocks has a better chance of going up rather than down because prices in general are rising. Conversely, if prices generally are falling, then purchasing a stock in that environment is not nearly as productive even if the stock you purchase is a very bullish stock.

---

[15] O'Brien Tom, Timing the Trade: How Price and Volume Move Markets, Tiger Financial News Network, Inc., 1st Printing 2005.

Table 3 provides a general guideline for determining the trading bias based on the general market trends (short, intermediate, and long-term time frames).

Table 3 - General Market Trading Bias Matrix

Short Term	Intermediate Term	Long Term	Trading Bias
Bullish	Bullish	Bullish	Bullish
Bullish	Bullish	Sideways	Bullish
Bullish	Sideways	Bullish	Bullish
Sideways	Bullish	Bullish	Bullish
Bearish	Bullish	Bullish	Bullish
Bullish	Bearish	Bullish	Moderately Bullish
Bearish	Bearish	Bearish	Bearish
Bearish	Bearish	Sideways	Bearish
Bearish	Sideways	Bearish	Bearish
Sideways	Bearish	Bearish	Bearish
Bullish	Bearish	Bearish	Bearish
Bearish	Bullish	Bearish	Moderately Bearish
Sideways	Sideways	Sideways	Sideways
Sideways	Sideways	Bearish	Sideways Leaning Bearish
Sideways	Sideways	Bullish	Sideways Leaning Bullish

Sideways	Bearish	Sideways	Sideways Leaning Bearish
Sideways	Bullish	Sideways	Sideways Leaning Bullish
Bearish	Sideways	Sideways	Sideways
Bullish	Sideways	Sideways	Sideways

Table 3 depicts only 19 of the 27 possible combinations because they are the only combinations that form a trading bias. All others combinations are too muddled to use for bias determination. The hypothetical trend shown in Figure 5 is not depicted in Table 3 because the trend is not clearly defined as up, down, or sideways. In such a market, we say that the general market trend is ambivalent. In an ambivalent market, you have to defer to the sector trend for guidance while keeping an eye on where and how the general market trend evolves over time.

Sector Trends

Although the general market trend is at the top of the trend food chain, sector trends do have significant influence as well. A sector is a group of related stocks. The relation between these stocks is generally based upon the primary product (goods and/or services) that those in the sector sell. For example, the financial sector sells financial products, while the technology sector sells technology related products. Sectors may also be comprised of sub-sectors. For example, within the technology sector there is the software technology sector and the semiconductor sector (to name just two).

Like the general market, the sector has a reasonable amount of influence on whether a stock tends to rise or fall in price. Referring back to Figure 5, this same visualization applies to the sector as well as to the general market. In other words, both the general market and the various sectors each have independent trends for each of the possible time frames *at the same time*.

Unlike the general market which comprises **all** stocks that trade on a given exchange, stock sectors have an importance ranking within them. Stock sectors are not created equal. Some sectors are larger in size which makes their influence on the overall market greater. On the NYSE, for example, the financial sector is extremely important. If the financial sector is having trouble, it typically portends that the rest of the sectors are either having trouble or soon will. This is true since the financial sector is the companies that service all other companies that comprise the NYSE market. Most charting services allow you to track each sector of a given market. The financial sector is generally accepted as being represented by the banking index (BKX).

In the NASDAQ, you essentially have the same situation where the semiconductor sector (tracked through the SOX index) represents the dominant sector.

In this age of technology and financing, if these two sectors are not going up, it is unlikely that the general market will be moving higher. Conversely, if both are moving down, it is likely that the general market will be under pressure to move lower as well.

Another caveat is that the importance of sectors is not static. In the current market environment, for example, the energy sector has grown in importance over the past few years. In fact (at the time of this writing), it has grown to the point where it is the largest sector weighting in the S&P 500. However, note these sector relationships do change over time.

When forming a trading bias, it is important to consider not only the general market, but the dominant sectors as well. Remember these guidelines:

1. Start with the big picture – what phase of the market cycle is the market in?
2. Review the general market trends for those indexes that you trade.
3. Examine the trends of the dominant sectors in each of those general markets.

What you are looking for is the convergence or divergence of these various inputs in order to formulate a picture of general market health. In doing this, you have the making of a tradable trading bias. This bias will guide you in the decision we asked at the beginning of this chapter, "Is *any* stock worth purchasing?"

If your analysis leads you to a bullish bias, then the answer is "yes." If the analysis leads you to a bearish bias, then the answer is "no." If no, then you should focus on the short sell of stocks rather than purchasing them. If the bias is neither bullish nor bearish but sideways, consider the idea of buying towards the bottom of the trading range and selling near the top.

Recognize that a clear-cut bias does not always develop. Sometimes it is ambiguous. When that happens, we say that the bias is weak or altogether unappealing at this particular time. Recognize that there are times when the market is not generally tradable (at least not profitably). During these times it is not in your best interest to force trades.

As a trader, what you are looking for is to have the greatest probability of success on your side when entering a trade. That provides you with the highest probability of individual success. You can't force the market to support your desire to trade a particular stock or stock sector. Instead you have to *listen* to the market. You have hear what it is saying. If, through trend analysis, you determine that now is not a particularly good time to trade, then respect it. Remember, the market is cyclical and eventually the market will provide you will a higher probability of success – you just have to be patient.

6

Trade Idea Generation

O nce you have your trading bias and are ready to make some trades, how do you find stocks that are the best buys or short sells at this particular time? How do you get started?

In order to trade, you must possess trading ideas. There are many ways to obtain ideas, but given the advent of the Internet and the information revolution, the most efficient way currently available to the *little guy* is through the use of stock screeners. There are many types of screeners, but to use any of them and to trade in general, you have to embrace the technology that is today's trading landscape.

Embrace the Technology

So much has changed over the past fifteen years in the trading world. Fifteen years ago, you most likely had to use a live broker to trade – someone on the other end of the phone. If you were reasonably active, you would have likely talked to your broker enough to know them on a first-hand basis. The commission costs you paid (not counting the slippage costs[16] that you probably incurred), would have far exceeded the prices you pay today. That was the cost you incurred in order to have someone to talk to.

Although it is cheaper to talk with a broker today, it is still much more costly than if you do it yourself using the Internet[17]. Nowadays you can buy and sell securities safely and instantaneously via an online broker. The prices you pay are as cheap as a penny per share. Fifteen years ago, it would easily have cost you a dollar a share. What a difference a decade and a half makes!

This revolution in access and transaction costs transpired as a result of two important events that occurred in the early 70's. In 1974, the Securities and Exchange Commission (SEC) mandated a 13-month trial in the deregulation of brokerage commission costs.

---

[16] As described previously, slippage costs are those extra costs that you incur. Many times it is the result of the brokerage firm or the market maker likely pocketing a few dollars on the order because you specified a market order in haste to exit the position providing them with the opportunity to do so.

[17] Almost all major brokerage houses do business on the Internet nowadays. From Charles Schwab to Bank of America – there are a myriad of brokerages that are willing and waiting to serve you through the Internet. Each provides a trading platform and a various set of tools.

That trial led to the first discount brokerage, Charles Schwab, where commission costs were dramatically reduced. During this same time frame, the NASDAQ rolled out their Small Order Execution System (SOES). SOES provided the automatic execution of small order lots. This system would prove to be huge, in the grand scheme of things. The combination of discount brokers and SOES resulted in continued and significant price reductions for years. These events dramatically reduced the incremental transaction cost of trading.

Consider that if your cost per share on a $10 stock is one penny versus one dollar, the incremental costs are monumental. In the former case, you need the stock to move just one cent to break even while in the latter case, you need it to move a whole dollar. In the high cost world, the stock would have to move ten percent just to break even – a feat all the more daunting because many stocks don't even move ten percent in a year. Of course, these high costs were bore by the small traders, since large institutional traders received preferred treatment and prices. This difference in price is tremendous and was the primary reason that small traders simply did not participate in the stock market in the 70's. Those few investors who did purchase stocks bought and held them for many years. That was the mindset then and remains the mindset – even now.

With the cost of buying and selling stocks dramatically reduced, the remaining obstacle to the adoption of active trading by small traders was that of access. When the Internet was embraced in the early 1990s, brokerages catering to small traders emerged. Although it took a few years to work out the software connectivity, reliability, and platform security issues, the result was that the small trader's revolution finally began to materialize. The move by brokerages to tap into mainstream America's desire to trade securities provided a far more fertile trading ground for the small trader. The combination of lowered transaction costs, easy trading access, and ubiquitous access to trading information has finally bridged the gap between large and small traders.

For the first time in the history of securities trading, the playing fields are nearing a level of fairness that makes the trading field of yesteryear seem as archaic and out-of-date as today's cars make the horse and buggy era seem. The opportunity for a small trader to be a successful trader is truer now than ever before. The opportunity for an individual to take their financial success into their own hands is a reality.

If the view is broadened to include the additional needs of a trader beyond trading access, one can see that there also is a revolution in the services available. I can remember when I used to wait for the Wall Street Journal's arrival around midmorning to look and see what the previous day's closing price, volume, and open interest were on commodity contracts I was trading. Needless to say, I was at quite a disadvantage as I didn't have access to timely information.

With the ubiquitous and instantaneous nature of the Internet, traders now enjoy the timely receipt of data and information. Most online brokers offer real time streaming quotes for free, while a fair number offer high-powered trading stations as part of their services.

Charting systems used to be expensive and somewhat outdated. Now they are free, online, and updated not only daily, but updated real time. The various technical indicators that a technician uses are available and provided on a real time basis as well. These charting services have more technical measures than one could ever hope to learn, let alone use (see www.prophet.net as an example). Numerous web sites, both for profit and free, are available and devoted to fundamental and technical analysis. News feeds are provided live through brokerages, as well as through public sites such as MarketWatch (http://www.marketwatch.com).

The changes in the trading landscape are remarkable and unavoidable. Fast, reasonably priced, or even free information is now available to the *little guy*. In fact, the most significant problem facing a trader nowadays is information overload rather than the lack thereof. Your success depends on keeping it simple. In most cases, less is more.

Love it or hate it, technology is no longer an option for a small trader; it's a requirement. Embrace the technology. It levels the playing field and makes you successful on the trading gridiron.

Stock Screeners – What are they?

A stock screener is a tool that traders can use to filter stocks based on selected criterion. Stock screeners are used, because they are simple and efficient. There are over 7,000 stocks available to trade on the three major U.S. exchanges (the NYSE, the NASDAQ, and the AMEX). With that many stocks available to trade, there are way too many stocks to try to track. Considering the fact that you want to be invested in one or more stocks that have the greatest opportunity of returning a profit (for the time frame you are trading), you should consider enlisting the help of stock screeners to *uncover* those stocks that are ready to move. So exactly how do you use a stock screener?

A stock screening tool provides a trader the ability to specify a strict set of criteria to filter through all the specified stocks for desired matches. For example, you could screen stocks by entering the following criteria:

- Listed on the NYSE
- Related to the telecommunications industry
- Have a P/E (profit to earnings ratio) between 15 and 25
- Have an annual Earnings per Share growth rate of at least 15% for the past three years

Given these instructions, the stock screener produces a list of stocks that meet these specific criteria. In this particular example, the stock screener is used to screen the universe of stocks using four fundamental criteria (most screeners allow both technical and fundamental criteria to be specified). The sophistication and variability of stock screeners is dependent on the screener. There are free screeners available on the Internet; others available from select brokers if you open an account with them; and others that can be purchased on a pay-as-you-go basis. A simple search for *stock screeners* on the Internet produces a large list of possibilities. Visit www.tatoday.com for a list that I have found useful.

Over time you will develop your own screening criteria. Mostly it is trial and error. If the screening criteria you use results in too many ideas, then you should add more screening criteria or increase the strictness of the current search criteria to narrow the matches. If it is too restrictive, remove some of the screening criteria. Eventually you will end up with a set of screening criteria that provides you with a constant stream of ideas. It's similar to using Yahoo or Google to do an Internet search. If you have too many options, you refine your search criteria to narrow the results.

Select at least one stock screener. It is well worth the effort invested in learning how to use these tools because it easily replaces several days' worth of work with a few clicks of a mouse.

Determining What to Screen For

Once you settle on a particular stock screener, the next issue is what criteria should be used. The answer to that question will probably solidify over time but to a large part, the answer will be found in your approach to trading.

One typical trading strategy is to find a strong stock and trade in the direction of the prevailing trend. One example of such a trade would be to find a stock that is breaking out to new highs. If you find a good one, then you simply buy it and hang on for the ride. Here's an example of what that looks like on a chart:

Figure 6 – ANO; A Breakout to New Highs

As you can see in Figure 6, there was a defined area of old highs around $1.25. Once ANO broke through those highs, it was just a matter of buying the stock and holding on. If you have any experience in trading stocks, you probably have some ideas about some screening conditions you might want to use.

Here's a simple scanning criteria that would alert you to a chart like that depicted in Figure 6.

- Listed on the NYSE or the NASDAQ or the AMEX
- Have hit a new 52-week high

The problem with the above scan and with others like it is that there are times when buying breakouts (like the one illustrated in Figure 6) work well, and then there are times when they don't. This is true of all scanning criteria, not just breakouts. The reason that the results are uneven in terms of success is that the stock you are trading is not traded in isolation. There are many factors that cause a stock to go up or down. It is a combination of the company itself, how other companies in that particular industry sector are doing, and a result of how the general stock market is doing. As we previously discussed in the section on Time Frames and Trends, a rising tide lifts all boats while a receding tide tends to lower them all. Once you realize that some screens will do better in some market environments and less so in others, you are that much farther ahead. This knowledge will enable you to use your trading bias to dictate the screening criteria you use which matches the trading bias you have developed.

Returning to the question of how you find *good screening ideas*, the answer is actually pretty simple – keep it simple. Concentrate on what's most important in your trading like. It might be a new 52 week high, a jump in volume simultaneous with price, or maybe just a jump or fall in price coincident with an earnings release. The key is to find some set of criteria that yields potential trade setups on the trading time frame you have an interest in trading and that also is in harmony with your trading bias for the market *for that same time frame.*

To elucidate, take two extremes. In one extreme, if the general market and the sector that you have interest in are bullish across all time frames (see Figure 7), then a screen for bullish breakout technical patterns would make sense.

Figure 7 – Bullish General Market and Sector Price Trend Cube

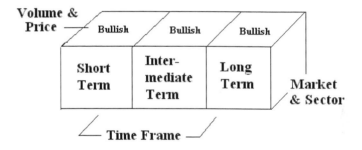

The other extreme, might be where the general market and the sector that you have interest in are bearish across all time frames (see Figure 8). In that case, a screen for bullish breakout technical patterns would **not** make sense; in fact, it would be a bit suicidal.

Figure 8 – Bearish General Market and Sector Price Trend Cube

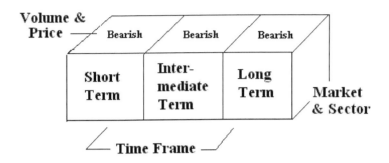

The importance of changing your screening criteria as your trading bias changes is an important one and should be adhered to when generating ideas for future trades.

What follows are a couple of more advanced screening criteria to illustrate how you might find particular technical patterns. This can be used anytime the general market appears to be in an intermediate-term bullish advance and when you are searching for stocks that are exhibiting bullishness. The screening criteria for this scan are:

- Exchanges: NYSE, AMEX, NASDAQ(NM)
- Average Volume is at least 50,000 shares
- Last Price is above 50-Day MA

- Virtual Volume is at least 200% greater than Average Volume
- Last Price is at least $2

The above criteria attempts to identify stocks that:

- Have traded on above average volume
- Are liquid stocks (not a bulletin board/penny stock)
- Are likely short to intermediate-term time frame bullish (trading above the 50 day moving average).

The following is another example of a scan that can be used in a bullish market. It seeks to exploit the up and down nature of a market advance by searching for retraces in strong stocks over a short term time frame. The screening criteria for this bullish retrace scan are:

- Exchanges: NYSE, AMEX, NASDAQ(NM)
- Average Volume is at least 50,000 shares
- Volume is at least 50% less than Average Volume (30 day MA)
- Last Price is greater than 2
- Last Price is below 20-Day Moving Average
- Last Price is above 50-Day Moving Average
- Last Price is within 10% of 52-Week High
- Last Price is above 200-Day Moving Average
- Last Price is within 10% of Lifetime High

This scan attempts to identify stocks that have advanced strongly, but now are pulling back. The reasoning for this lies in the desire to buy stocks at a point where you can reduce your risk of error. If you are wrong, and the stock really has finished moving higher, then you want to be able to exit without losing much capital. In other words, you try to buy the stock as it *retraces* back towards its reversion mean. Figure 9 illustrates an example of the type of chart that this scan identifies.

Figure 9 - An Example of a Retrace Scan Result (Mastercard)

Notice how MasterCard, has recently retraced under its 20 day moving average, but is still trading above the 50

and 200 day moving average. All of these criteria were specified in the scanning criteria. The results of this scan are a group of stocks that are retracing much like the one in this example.

In summary, what you are scanning for is dependent to a great degree on what opportunities the market is offering. The opportunities change all the time and your job is to stay in synchronicity with those changes in order to be successful.

Managing Trading Ideas

One of the more common misconceptions that newer traders have, is the expectation for the perfect scan – a scan that provides you with three winners from the universe of stocks that exist. Unfortunately, there is no such scan. The reality is that you will have to sift through fifty charts for every three or four that have a good opportunity to succeed. Even then, of the three or four gems that you find, only one or two may actually be tradable in the current time frame. The vast majority of stocks that you uncover with your scans are probably not ready to buy or short sell[18] at the time you find

---

[18] A short sell is a method of selling a stock that you do not own. Essentially you *borrow* the stock from someone who does own it and then sell it to a third party. Your broker handles all the details of borrowing and returning the shares making the process as simple as buying a stock.

them. They may take another couple of days to develop or even a few weeks.

If you run your scans daily and find an average of five stocks a day, then by the end of the week you will have twenty five stocks that you are monitoring. In a couple weeks you're up to fifty, and in three weeks you are overloaded and have lost interest. You don't care to scan anymore because you can't keep up with what you already have – information overload. To be effective, you need an efficient way to manage the stocks you do find.

Watch List Management

Every good trader has to develop a method for managing his potential trades. Usually this is done through watch lists. Watch lists are nothing more than a list of stocks you watch. You essentially keep an eye on stocks that you have previously identified as having the potential to trade *if* they develop the way you want them to. For example, you might find a stock that has broken out to new highs and you want to keep an eye on it to see if it retraces back to the breakout area so you can purchase it. You don't want to purchase it yet, but if it retreats some in price it may be worth it; so you add it to your watch list.

Most charting services allow you to easily set up scans as well as watch lists to track potential trading candidates over time. When choosing such a service, the key desirable features are the ability to:

- Have multiple lists
- Easily move a stock from one list to another
- Quickly examine the stocks in those lists

The common factor between all the stocks on your watch list is time. Given this, it makes a lot of sense to organize the stocks in terms of time. For example, create two watch lists, *immediate* and *future*. Place the potential stocks you find into one of these two groups. In doing this, you have the beginnings of a simple watch list management method. Examine the *immediate* watch list daily, adding to and removing from the list as conditions change for each stock. The *future* watch list you look at less frequently. By managing the lists based on time frames, you have rudimentary yet functional way to keep your lists (and thus your ideas) fresh. As the charts change over time, you either move stocks from the *immediate* list to the *future* list or vice versa. If a stock loses its appeal, remove the stock completely from both.

Once you get this basic list management down, augment it. For example, you could add a couple longer term lists of stocks that are long-term bullish and long-term bearish. Once a month or so, flip through these two lists looking to see if any of the stocks may be short-term tradable. If so, move them to the *immediate* or *future* lists. If they are no longer long-term bullish or long-term bearish, then remove them from the list. The end result is that, over time, you add new stocks to your watch lists as you discover them via scanning and you remove them during your review process when searching for stocks that are ready to trade.

Managing Alarms

Another useful management technique is the use of alarms. As a small trader, it is quite common to have ten or twenty stocks that are simultaneously within a few cents or dollars of an entry point. Most small traders do not have the time to sit around and watch the trading screen all day long; they typically have a day time job and trade in their spare time. One way to time your entry well, yet free yourself from monitoring the stock all day, is to set an alarm for the stock.

Although you could just place a limit order into the market to purchase or short sell the security that is close to the price you have decided to trade it at, there are a couple of problems with doing so. The first is "What are you going to do if you have many stocks that you place limit orders for and most of the orders execute?" The result could be that you have purchased more stock than you wished to. Since you don't know which ones may or may not trigger the purchase via a limit order, it's a bit of a guessing game that may leave you with too many stock positions.

The second and more serious problem is fast price movement. Consider the case where you are looking to buy stock XYZ at the price point of $20? You put a limit order in and, while you are busy doing your real work, the order is triggered. Unfortunately, the price continues to drop and by the end of the day, XYZ is trading at $16. Some piece of news caused the stock to plummet and now you are in for the ride; like it or not.[19]

To avoid these potential problems, use alarms to notify you when the entry price is within reach and to notify you of when you should exit a trade once entered. Most trading stations allow you to do this. You can set an alarm based on the current bid or ask price[20]; the last price that the stock was sold for; etc. When a stock that you have been waiting for begins to approach the price where you believe it would be a good purchase or short sell, using an alarm to notify you represents a time-saving notification strategy that lets you time your entry efficiently and safely. The same is true of notification to exit a position.

---

[19] It is true that some trading platforms allow you to enter a stop that is conditional with the entry order, so that you can protect against this case, but some do not.

[20] The *bid* is the price that someone is willing to pay for a stock while *ask* is the price that someone is current willing to sell a stock for.

Trading Tools

A rmed with ideas from your stock screening tools, you are now ready to execute and manage the trade. Just like an auto mechanic whose toolbox reveals the tools of their trade, the stock trader wields a set of tools that they use in trading stocks. To some degree, I have already talked about a number of tools in the trader's toolbox. The most basic of tools is the computer itself. Trading and computers go hand in hand. The applications you use on the computer make up the additional tool set (such as the charting service and the news feeds). Stock screeners and watch lists make up another group, just like pliers and screwdrivers round out the auto-mechanics tool box.

All of the trader's tools discussed so far are used in preparation of the trade. Another class of tools is the trading platform and the particular trading orders used to make purchases and sales. The trading platform you choose should be simple to use, yet reliable and able to offer consistently fast executions for the trades you execute. It is highly desirable to have a trading platform that does not result in your order being *screened* or *bundled* by your broker before being sent to the exchange for execution. This added delay can cost you via higher execution costs as a result of slippage or bad fills within the brokerage itself[21].

As for the tools to place orders to buy and sell stocks, most brokers offer the majority of the order types discussed below. These order types are based either on price, time, or a combination of both. Many of the orders you use, or will use, are a combination of both time and price.

Given that there are a number of order mechanisms available to the stock trader, which ones you use depends on what type of trader you are and what you are trading. As with anything, you probably should start out simple and add complexity as you advance in your

---

[21] Many broker order systems have validation and bundling services built into them. For example, when you place an order with this type of firm, rather than having your order move directly to the floor of the exchange, it is instead routed to the broker first. There, the brokerage has software that typically does some validation of your order and many times attempts to fill your order within their brokerage rather than sending it to the floor. If they can do so, the result is that they make the full fee without giving it to the exchange. This is good for the broker but it can be bad for you. If it is a market order, for example, you can end up getting a fill of the order within the brokerage firm without ever having the possibility of getting a better fill within the broader market.

trading endeavors. The simplest orders are day only limit and market orders. They provide you with the bulk of what you need.

Time Orders

Orders based on time are used to instruct your broker about how long you want an order to be active.

Good till Cancelled Orders

Good-till-cancelled orders are those orders that do not expire at the end of the normal hours on the day that they were placed. This type of order instructs your broker to keep the order active until you explicitly cancel it. Many brokers will place a time limit on a *good-till-cancelled order* of two or three months to prevent having stale orders executing some time in the future after having been long forgotten.

Day Orders

A *day order* is just what it sounds like; an order that has to be executed on the day it is issued. If the order remains after normal market hours have completed (see the next section), the order is automatically cancelled. If you want to put the order in for more than a day, you either have to place it each day using a *day order* or place it as a *good-till-cancelled order* as explained above.

After Hours Orders

The equity markets have normal market trading hours as well as before and after hours when stocks are also tradable. Historically, there were only normal market hours, but as the financial revolution continues, the NYSE, NASDAQ, and other exchanges now allow trading outside the normal hours. Trading now occurs a few hours before and after normal market hours. These additional periods of time are called the *before and after hours* markets (for lack of a better name). To trade them you must issue trading orders that specifically authorize trades in these less liquid market conditions.

Because the after hours markets are less liquid, you definitely do not want to use *market orders* (see below) in that trading environment because the order price could be horrendous. In fact, until you have traded for a while, you should probably *ignore the before and after hours markets.*

Stock Entry and Exit Orders

Market Orders

A *market order* is the simplest and quickest way to get your order filled. A *market order* instructs your broker to buy or sell the stock immediately at the prevailing price no matter what that price is when your order hits the trading floor (in some cases it is a physical trading floor but more and more it is an electronic one).

The danger in using this type of order is that in a volatile market, the price you receive on a *market order* can be hugely different from the price you see on your quote screen. The less liquid the stock, the less useful a *market order* is because slippage costs climbs proportionally to the illiquidity of the stock. On the other hand, in a liquid market, the use of a *market order* is perfectly fine and results in immediate order execution. They are especially useful when exiting an existing position when the stock is moving in your favor. *Market orders* tend to be the cheapest priced order (brokerage cost) you can issue.

Limit Orders

Limit orders instruct your broker to buy or sell a stock at a particular price. The purchase or sale does not occur unless the market price matches your limit price. In fact, you are only guaranteed execution if the stock trades above (on a sell order) or below (on a buy order). For example, if you instruct your broker to purchase 200 shares of General Motors at $13, you are guaranteed that if you make the purchase, it will be at $13 or better ($13 or less). A *limit order* gives you control over your entry or exit point by fixing the price. *Limit orders* are preferable for entering into a position, but not necessarily for exiting one.

The potential problem with a *limit order* is that you may or may not have your order filled depending on whether the stock trades at the limit price you specify. A further problem is that even if the stock trades at the limit price you specify, it still may or may not get executed. The reason for this is that there are times (though reasonably rare) where a stock will trade at the limit price, but only a portion of the shares available to trade at that price actually trade (and they may not be your shares).

Generally speaking, for illiquid stocks, a *limit order* is ideal for stock entry. In fact, if the bid to ask[22] spread is large, you typically would never want to use a *market order*.[23]

---

[22] In a stock exchange, there are orders to purchase stocks and orders to sell stocks. When trying to purchase, a buyer *bids* on the stock. When trying to sell a stock, the seller *asks* for a certain price to sell out. That's where the terms *bid* and *ask* come from. The *bid to ask spread* is simply the difference in price between what someone is willing to sell as opposed to what someone is willing to pay for a given stock (or for any financial instrument for that matter).

[23] For every stock, there is a price where a willing purchaser *bids* for the stock. Conversely, there will be a price where a willing seller will *ask* to sell the stock. The difference between these two price points is referred to as *the bid/ask spread*.

All or None Orders

All or none orders state that you want the entire order to execute or none at all. For example, if you are trying to buy 1000 shares of XYZ Corporation and you want either all of the shares or none of the shares, you would issue an *all or none order*. These orders are typically used in conjunction with a *market on close order* where you want to make sure you get all the shares at the close of the day. For a small trader, this is probably overkill.

Market on Close

The *market on close* order is used to buy or sell shares at the closing price of the day. It is unlikely you would use this type of order, though it is available from most brokers.

One Cancels the Other

The *one cancels the other* order consists of two orders that are joined together. When one executes, the other is cancelled. This type of order is usually used in two differing circumstances:

- Buying a breakout or a breakdown in a stock
- Maintaining both a target price and stop order simultaneously

In the former case, an example would be that a stock has been trading for a long time between $10 and $11. As a result, there are probably lots of buy stop orders at the top of the range ($11), and a lot or sell stop orders at the bottom of the range ($10). In that case, you could potentially profit by buying the stock when it *breaks higher* or by selling the stock when it *breaks lower*. A *one cancels the other* order is ideal for such a structured trade.

In the latter case, if attempting to exit a stock at your target price but wanting to maintain your stop loss order until you exit, the use of a *one cancels the other* order at both your target and stop prices is ideal. If one executes, the other is immediately removed from the order queue.

Risk Management Orders

Another class of tools includes those orders that you use to protect your positions. These tools are critical tools – tools that are invaluable in your trading needs. *Stop loss orders* are critical to your success as a trader.

Stop Loss (Market) Orders

Stop loss orders are generally used as protection tools although they do have a function as entry tools as well. Traders use the *stop loss market order* to instruct their broker to either buy or sell a security at the market if the trigger price is hit.

If you previously purchased a stock and are placing a *stop loss order* as a protection order, then you would issue the order below the current price. If the stock price falls to the specified price point, the *stop loss order* becomes a *market sell order* and your broker sells the stock immediately at the prevailing price.

In the case of a short sell of a stock, if you are placing a *stop loss order* as a protection order, then you would issue the order above the current price. If the stock price rises above the specified price point, then the *stop loss order* becomes a *market buy order* and your broker buys back the stock immediately at the prevailing price.

In the above two scenarios, view the stop loss order as an insurance order … it ensures that you will exit if the price you specify is violated. It is a way to control risk.

The *stop loss order* may be used when establishing a position as well. For example, there might be a situation where you want to buy a stock if it crosses some threshold higher than it is now. In such a case, you could place a *stop buy order* at an entry price that is higher than the current price. In that case, the order would only execute if the stock price moves up far enough to trigger the order initiating a purchase of the stock. The same is true of entering a stock via a short sell using the *stop loss sell order*.

Stop Loss (Limit) Orders

A *stop loss limit order* is exactly the same as the *stop loss market order* with the exception that you specify a limit price in addition to the trigger price. For example, a *stop loss limit sell order* might have a trigger at $30. This indicates to the broker that if the price reaches $30, your order should be triggered. The second part of the specification is the minimum that you will sell the stock for once the $30 level is hit. For example, if you specify a limit of $29.75 then once $30 is hit your *stop loss sell order* would trigger. If the price was still at or above $29.75, then the stock would be sold as instructed at the prevailing price at or above $29.75. If unable to fill immediately, then the order would trigger but the actual execution would only happen if and when the price moved back to $29.75 or greater. If the price never moved back to $29.75 or higher, then the order execution would not occur; only the trigger.

Limit orders are useful in stocks where stock liquidity is limited and the bid/ask spread is large. They are more risky because, even though you want to exit your position, you are not guaranteed to do so if the prices move too fast once your stop is triggered. If you use *limit orders,* then you need to at least keep an occasional eye on the market during trading hours in case your order triggers but does not execute.

Trailing Orders

Trailing orders are a way for you to have a *stop loss/gain order* that moves with the market while trading is occurring. You typically use it to protect a profit once a profit has been obtained.

The usual situation is where you have gains in the stock you are protecting, but you believe that you may obtain further gains if you simply remain patient and allow the market to continue to work in your favor. However, you do not want to lose all of those gains if the stock were to move against you, thus you issue a *trailing stop order* that either is based on some fixed price or percentage amount. For example, you could place a *trailing stop order* 50¢ from the current trading price. As the price moves up, the trailing stop order moves up to remain 50¢ from the highest traded price. If the price moves down 50¢ from the highest price recorded that day, it will trigger your *stop loss sell order*. This results in a *market sell order* to liquidate the specified number of shares at the prevailing price. The same applies to a *trailing order* that is percentage based.

Partial Orders

There is nothing in the rule book that says that you have to buy or sell **all** the shares you intend to accumulate or liquidate at once. One of the more common mistakes in trading is that this is in fact what most people do. It's an all or nothing mentality that borders on lunacy since the likelihood that you buy or sell at exactly the right moment is about as unlikely as a pig flying. The reason for this tendency is historical; the transaction costs associated with buying and selling shares historically were too high to justify the use of multiple partial buys and sells for the *little guy*. This is no longer true. The transaction costs of making multiple transactions are a small pittance compared to the extra costs of buying everything at a higher price and then watching the price of your purchased stock fall further.

If you want to establish a position in a given stock, there is nothing to stop you from buying a third of the position now and the other two thirds later. Assuming you are so good or so lucky as to make the first purchase at the lowest cost, there's nothing wrong with adding additional shares later at a higher price. If what you expect to happen actually occurs, buying the stock as it continues to rise in price is sometimes justifiable.

The same is true of the exit. Again, timing the perfect exit is almost impossible. Instead, you have to be extremely lucky for this to happen. Multiple sales at varying prices are not only mentally preferable; they are more profitable to your portfolio over time as well. If you become used to making partial sells you will find that, over time, your portfolio ends up remaining closer to its highs rather than its lows because you are taking some profits off the table and putting them into your pocket as profits become available. Since the market never goes straight up or straight down, taking partial trading profits as the market ebbs and flows is an ideal way of managing your portfolio wealth as well as your portfolio risk!

Risk Management

T he management of risk is probably the most important concept that you have to fully grasp in order to be a successful trader; especially as the *little guy.* As a small trader, your portfolio size is limited and your ability to continually augment your portfolio with fresh influxes of capital is reasonably limited.

Pick up almost any trading book and the focus is either on the fundamental or technical aspect of trading. Sure, there are bits and pieces scattered around that address money and risk management, but for the most part, traders write books that dissect the fundamentals or that analyze the technical patterns. As a consequence, one finds little emphasis placed on money and risk management. That's really too bad because if you don't consider money management as a key part of your trading strategy, your likelihood of success is next to zero. The concept of money management can be divided into two fundamental paradigms; capital preservation and the trading strategies you employ to minimize risk.

Capital preservation as a concept embodies two separate thoughts:

- Shifting your focus from *creating profits*, **to instead** focus on *preventing significant losses in your investment capital.*
- Ensuring that the portfolio returns are at a rate that is at least equal to, but preferably more than the rate of inflation; but in all cases, positive.

> **Note that this reflects our earlier definition of a successful trader (refer to the Defining a Successful Trader section).**

How one achieves capital preservation while still operating as a successful trader is the dilemma facing all traders because they are somewhat conflicting goals. On one hand, you need to make more money than the average trader. On the other hand, you must do this without unduly risking your investment capital.

So how can you outperform without taking greater risks? Is it even possible? I would suggest that not only is it possible, it is probable as long as you actively consider risk as part of your overall strategy. Since risk is an inherent part of trading, you first have to consider what types of risk exists. Once you have a firm understanding of the risks that exist, only then can you consider implementing some of the risk reduction methods that are available to you while you trade. Finally, by coupling the risk reduction methods with a number of risk reducing trading strategies, you can actually outperform on a consistent basis while simultaneously practicing capital preservation.

Capital Preservation and Sources of Risk

A trader's capital is the lifeblood of their profession. Without capital, a trader cannot trade. Above all else, the small trader must seek to protect their capital. This is an area where the small trader and the larger trader differ greatly. A large trader, in particular, is a trader who manages other people's money (like a mutual fund for example) and can cope with a large drawdown on their capital – especially if the general market is suffering as well. Money managers working for established money management firms tend to have continual inflows of capital (they have huge advertising budgets that continually bring in new money) that allow them to continue averaging into positions at lower and lower price points. As long as the money keeps coming, they keep buying. Unless the market never goes back up, their strategy eventually will work. It's a replay of the casino example discussed earlier.

Mutual funds also have other attributes that reinforces their "buy low and keep buying lower" behavior. In particular, they are monolithic due to size and in most cases, they trade long only (i.e., they typically do not short sell stocks). As a result, in a down market, their goal is to lose less than their counterparts and the S&P 500. That's how they define success. They measure their success on a relative basis, irregardless of whether they actually make or lose money.

A small trader, on the other hand, generally cannot suffer a large capital drawdown and still be successful. The measure of their success is starkly different. Your money is real and there is a big difference between making more and losing what you have. In many cases, it represents your income as well. It's not funny money. A loss of 20% requires a subsequent gain of 25% just to get even again. The strategies you employ **must**, I repeat, **must** consider capital preservation as a key in achieving success as defined.

So how much of a drawdown is allowed? Is a 10% drawdown acceptable? How about 20%? Again, there's no *right* answer. Think of it in a different way. Personally I keep track of my portfolio gains and losses on a daily basis. I always have my all time high (for the portfolio) in sight. Although I look to make gains everyday, there are definitely times where simply staying close to the all the time highs while repositioning the portfolio is a success. A solid way to measure your short-term success is to stay within 5% of your all time highs. If you allow yourself to believe that a 20% or 30% drawdown is appropriate, then you have a different measure of success than I'm proposing. A large variability in your gains and losses over time represents one of two things; either you are a lousy trader and portfolio manager, or your risk tolerance is much higher than it should be as a small trader. Slow and steady is the approach that offers lower risk and longer term rewards. There is nothing wrong with taking a little more time to get to your wealth destination if, in the process of achieving that wealth, you increase your odds of actually getting there.

If you stay within 5% of your all time highs, you are always within striking distance of new highs. If you fall back much further than that, you will either fail in your endeavors or begin taking greater risks to reach your success measures. Increased risk intensifies your chance of failure. That's a fact.

In order to successfully preserve your capital, consider how it can be lost. The following are the primary types of risk along with mitigation strategies.

Overnight Risk

Overnight risk refers to the risk you take when holding any securities while the market for those securities is closed. Historically the markets were closed overnight, thus the term *overnight risk* was coined[24]. If the market is closed, you have no opportunity to trade the securities; hence the risk. If something was to happen during the period when the markets were closed and it materially devalued the securities you held, you would have no opportunity to do anything about it. If something very bad happened, you could lose a lot of money.

One way to avoid overnight risk is to not hold anything during that period of time where the market for that security is closed. There are traders who in fact do just that. Such a posture would require you to be a day trader, which is not a strategy that most would choose to pursue and is not one that I would advocate for most traders. It may be appealing in some ways, but practically speaking, it is probably not a viable path for the *little guy* due to the excessive time demands.

A more practical way to mitigate risks would be to offset (hedge) your positions prior to the market closing. For example, if you purchased a few gold stocks, you could take a short sell position in a basket of gold stocks to *protect* your positions while the markets are closed. This strategy is commonly referred to as hedging. Hedging is not without its own set of

---

[24] Anymore markets are open for longer periods of time and some markets are virtually open all the time trading most everyday, all day and night (except weekends).

problems though, because it is highly unlikely that you will find a basket of securities that are an exact match of those you already have. Even if you did find an exact match, you would still have the issue of having to decide when to remove the hedge as well. For example, say you hedged your long positions in gold stocks with a short on a basket of gold stocks. The following day, once the market begins trading again, you find that the hedge trade you established is now losing money. What do you do? Do you hold the short (hedge) positions until they are profitable or sell them for a loss? Do you just wait and see what happens?

Hedging may sound like a simple and easy solution to mitigate overnight risk, but in reality it carries with it some degree of complexity once established. In many ways, it simply complicates the picture. What seemed simple instead becomes complex. In reality, overnight risk, for the most part, is just something you have to live with in most cases. There are times that hedging your positions may make sense, but not on a daily basis. Personally, I hedge positions occasionally. I usually do this when the positions I'm hedging have moved too far and too fast. The expectation is that the market could move against my existing positions yet I do not want to liquidate those positions – so I hedge them.

Using the gold stocks as an example once more, assume you have a reasonable profit in some existing gold stocks and that gold itself has moved higher each and every day for two or three weeks. You know that the farther the market stretches higher in a short period of time, the more and more likely it is that it will suffer some sort of pull back. Assuming the long term trend is higher and that you do not want to sell your stocks, hedging is a reasonable alternative.

In such a situation, you could begin to short a basket of gold stocks (like the GDX) or even short gold itself as a hedge. The risk is that you are wrong and gold just heads higher and higher without pulling back. In such a situation, your short position on the GDX or on gold (GLD) ends up acting as the premium on an insurance policy.

If your timing is good though, you may get exactly what you were looking for: a profit on the short hedge positions while your long positions decrease in value. In this case, you eventually take the profits on the short hedge position while maintaining your long positions.

With this sort of strategy, overnight risk is effectively zero if you are fully hedged or something approaching zero. All in all, this is a strategy that has its place. It is particularly useful in the more extreme situations where a market has moved so far and so fast that the odds of it reversing creates increased overnight risk.

Another way to mitigate overnight risk is to simply reduce your positions modestly as risk increases. Since markets typically do not move straight up or straight down for extended periods of time, when you do find yourself in a situation where your trades have profited greatly in a short period of time because of straight line move, take partial profits and reduce your risk[25].

Finally, probably the best mitigation strategy is to hold both long and short sell positions simultaneously in your portfolio. Overnight risk tends to affect all stocks, not just some sectors. So, if you have long positions in one sector and short sell positions in another and if something bad were to happen overnight, your long positions would lose while your short sell positions would gain.

Overnight risk is not an easily managed risk – at least not completely. As we all know (or at least should know), each trade carries risk whether you recognize it or not. Risk is always present in trading, that's just the nature of the game. The key is that you recognize it and take steps to minimize it when it becomes too great. The majority of the time, there is little you can do to reduce overnight risk (with the exception of holding a portfolio of long and short positions simultaneously; a strategy talked about later in the section titled *Mixing Long and Short Positions in a Portfolio*).

---

[25] Note in the case where a straight line move works against you, overnight risk is typically not a problem because you will end up stopping out of your positions due to having been incorrect about the direction of the trades you have placed.

Leverage Risk

Leverage is something the *little guy* should avoid most of the time – at least until you have traded for a sufficiently long enough period of time to perfect your risk management skills. Until then, it is too much of a gamble using your hard earned money. Essentially, leverage is where you borrow from your broker or banker in order to take on larger positions than you otherwise could have based on the amount of capital in your portfolio. There are three problems associated with leveraging – all of which make leveraging less palatable.

1. In most cases, there is a cost associated with leveraging[26]. For example, most brokerage firms allow a trader to trade up to one and a half to two times the value of their account. For example, if the value of your account is $10,000 and you want to buy $20,000 worth of stock, the broker will extend credit to you in order to do so. In return, they charge you interest on any monies you borrow. As a result, your costs increase and the returns that you generate must now increase sufficiently to cover the interest

---

[26] Some of the newer ETF (Exchange Traded Funds) products provide leverage at a marginal management fee cost. Additionally, if you trade futures contracts there isn't a cost to leverage since futures contracts are heavily leveraged inherently.

charges incurred. Otherwise, you are effectively losing money.

2. The broker issues margin calls (a situation where the broker requires you to add money to your account) if the assets you have purchased decrease too much in value. They do this to protect themselves because they have already loaned you money to trade and their collateral is at risk. Brokers are very tough about margin calls[27].

3. Leverage increases the potential for both higher returns and losses. Remember risks are what you are always attempting to control in trading. Increased risk forces you to tighten your stops to maintain the same overall portfolio risk percentages. The result of tighter stops is that your risk of being stopped out of a trade due to noise increases. In other words, leverage many times results in the trader incurring increased trade failures. If, as part of leveraging, you decide not to maintain your overall portfolio risk percentages, you are breaking a cardinal rule of trading which is to **never** put yourself in

---

[27] When a broker issues a margin call, you must deposit a sufficient amount of capital to bring your balance back up to the minimum that your broker requires. You usually have to do this overnight which incurs additional wiring costs. If you are unable or unwilling to do so in the time allotted by your broker, your broker has the right to close as many positions as needed at their own discretion and at whatever the prevailing price is in order to raise your capital position to a point that they deem necessary.

a situation where you could lose all or a significant portion of your trading capital. Trading capital is something you have to protect with all your money management principals.

The real problem with leveraging is that most people leverage when they are in a losing position (which is deadly). Traders usually leverage because they do not have the discipline required to take a loss if the trade turns against them. They decide to buy more of the losing stock or simply add more money to the account so that they do not *have to sell.* Unsuccessful traders, large and small, find themselves trading on hope rather than on sound money management principals. Hope, unfortunately, is not a valid trading strategy. If you choose to leverage, you should do so with extreme caution and with a well thought out strategy of where you enter and where you exit if the trade does not turn out as expected.

Asset Class Risk

An asset class refers to the notion that there are multiple distinct assets available in the marketplace to invest your money (some related to others [correlated] while some not [negatively correlated]). Asset class risk occurs when the asset classes that you have purchased are highly correlated. Even though the assets purchased may seem to be separate and distinct, rather than reducing your risk, you have actually increased it.

For example, a dollar that is decreasing in value relative to other currencies tends to cause most commodity prices to increase over time. Your asset class risk would be higher if you were to concentrate your purchases strictly in gold, silver, oil, lumber, etc. In such a case, even though you had purchased many different assets, your asset class risk would be greater because all of the purchases were highly correlated.

Certainly if you happen to be right about the direction of the trades, and they were to move in your favor, it would be successful because all of them would produce profits. On the other hand, if they did not move in your favor, it is highly likely that all of them would move against you. Thus, your losses would multiply because all of them would lose at the same time and by like amounts.

Asset class risk is something you have to be aware of. Recognition is needed, not so much because you want to avoid it instead, but because you need to understand it. Knowing your *true* overall risk profile is important when examining your portfolio risk. The simplest way to keep track of your asset class risk is to monitor the positions you have for each of the market sectors (asset classes). You can do this via a spreadsheet you maintain yourself, or your broker may conveniently do this for you. Table 4 is an example of sector holdings (asset classes). It is the result of a simple program I have written to manage this task for myself and portfolios that I manage for others. Using data from my broker, I update it nightly and use it to help manage portfolio and asset class risk[28].

Table 4 – Sector and Total Holdings (Absolute and as a Percentage)

Industry Sector	Current Holdings	Sector Percentage Holdings
Communication Equipment	$605.83	7.98 %
Copper	$167.11	2.20 %
Gold	$3942.44	51.96 %
Industrial Metals/Mineral	$1463.67	19.29 %
Nonmetallic Mineral Mining	$584.59	7.70 %
Savings & Loans	$344.16	4.54 %
Semiconductor Equip/Matrl	$151.33	1.99 %
Silver	$170.38	2.25 %
Sporting Goods Stores	$157.84	2.08 %
Percentage Long Holdings	$7587.35	20.40 %
Percentage Short Holdings	$0.00	0.00 %
Percentage Cash Holdings		79.60 %

---

[28] The highlighted numbers are a technique I use to draw my attention to any sector where the total of that sector is greater than 4% of my invested portion of the portfolio.

110

Liquidity Risk

Not every stock or trading instrument trades the same amount of shares. As an example, if you look at Cisco (symbol CSCO), it currently averages some 50 million shares traded per day and is very *liquid*. This means you can easily get in and out of the stock without any significant slippage cost. The bid/ask spread is as small as a penny for actively traded shares like CSCO, and as much as fifty or sixty cents in less liquid stocks. Liquidity risk occurs when you own an illiquid stock and must exit immediately. In such a situation, you are at risk of a costly exit if that exit must be made in haste.

As a small trader, you have the advantage of trading less liquid stocks because you are not typically trading a large number of shares. A stock that trades twenty thousands shares per day with a bid/ask spread of as much as ten or fifteen cents actually offers you an advantage over the larger trader in most circumstances. As long as you don't put yourself in a position where you have to liquidate your position immediately, you can use the bid/ask spread and the illiquidity of the stock to your advantage. *Capture* the spread by putting a limit order at the top end of the bid/ask spread and wait for someone to *hit the asking* price. To successfully trade less liquid stocks put yourself in a position where you can liquidate on your own terms; not someone else's terms.

Time Risk

Technically speaking, there are three basic components that move stocks:

- Price
- Volume
- Time

Each of these components is integral to the overall direction of a stock, but the latter is particularly interesting as a part of the larger concept of risk. Freely traded financial instruments, like stocks, do not move up and down in a straight line; they ebb and flow. This somewhat erratic up and down movement is the noise factor in the market and is ever present. Random noise with regards to a stock's price is a risk you take each and every time you make a stock purchase or a short sell.

Time risk presents itself in two ways:

1. Opportunity costs. The longer you have your money tied up in a stock, then thee is less money to invest in other stocks.
2. The longer you hold a stock, the greater the likelihood you will suffer a large drawdown in your capital due to one of many possible factors (such as exogenous risks).

It is important to reduce both these risks by perfecting your entry timing. Look at any stock chart to see this fact. Despite this lack of regularity, there are time intervals during a stock's movement where the risk associated with an established position is either increasing or decreasing. Intrinsically this is known though there exists no mathematical models that adequately explain this behavior. Nevertheless, its implicit existence does provide an advantage to a trader. Consider the following example.

When a stock has been in a long-term bullish uptrend (not shown in this shorter term time frame on the following chart) but has recently been involved in a short-term decline on decreasing volume, the odds increase for a change in direction (see Figure 10 below).

Figure 10 - GES - Ripe for a Change in Direction

When I say the *odds increase,* I mean to imply that conditions are in place where, within a reasonably short period of time (a few days at most), the stock should either respond to the decreasing desire to sell and reverse higher or something will happen to force it lower. The key to success in such a trade is that you enter the stock at the point in time where your time risk is reduced to a minimum. Regardless of the direction the stock takes from this point forward, it is likely to do it *soon.*

As a small trader, it is your desire to purchase or short sell a stock before it moves. But remember, do this as closely as possible to the point *where it will move*. In so doing, you decrease the amount of time you have your capital tied up in a given trade and you reduce your overall time risks to a smaller interval.

Exogenous Risk

Exogenous risk is a risk that strikes without notice. For example, the 9/11 hijacking of passenger planes and the use of them as flying suicide bombs is not something that you can protect against as it came without any notice. If you held a significant amount of stock in your portfolio without any protection, then it was a worst case scenario for you. It was an exogenous risk realized outside normal market hours (overnight risk) leaving very few with the ability to quickly protect themselves. If you remember, the stock market closed for several days after that hideous event occurred. When it did reopen, stock prices fell dramatically.

Exogenous risks are always a possibility that can strike in the most egregious ways. The only two modes of protection against such risks for the *little guy* are holding mostly cash and/or having a portfolio that maintains both long and short exposure simultaneously. Because its timing is unknown, preparation is not a choice. If the exogenous risk manifests itself during market hours, it is always best to hedge or move at least some of your portfolio to cash as quickly as possible and re-evaluate the situation once the event risk is more fully understood.

Undercapitalization Risk

Although it may seem counterintuitive, an undercapitalized account can actually result in you taking more risk, not less. The reason for this lies in the way people think about trading and how they actually trade.

A Small Account just isn't Worth the Effort

One of the first things a small trader has to overcome is the fact that trading, like any other occupation, is a job – not a hobby. It takes time, preparation, patience, and fortitude. For a while, a small trader can get by on sheer desire and the excitement of learning a new discipline but, in the end, trading is about making money. If you are working with a starting capital base of $5000, for example, how much can you realistically make on that $5000? Let's assume you can make 20% (which is a very nice return and difficult to do on a consistent basis). With an account of that size, the effort and time it takes to trade successfully just isn't worth the $1000 gains to be had.

Working with an undercapitalized account inevitably leads to one or both of the immortal sins of trading.

Either you begin to take on larger and larger risks to get larger and larger returns to *make it monetarily worthwhile*, or you find that you are not willing to spend the time that is necessary to do the preparation work required to trade. The result is bad trades and lost capital. In both scenarios, what was a small account becomes an even smaller one. This usually leads to even greater trading sins and the loss of all your starting capital.

What is a Sufficiently Capitalized Account?

For the reasons stated above, you should not consider trading with an undercapitalized account unless your objective is to learn how to trade effectively and successfully rather than to make money. If you want to make money and that is your primary objective, there are a few factors to consider when determining what a sufficiently capitalized trading account is.

The first factor is that current SEC law identifies a frequent trader as a trader who exhibits what the SEC terms as a *pattern day trader*[29]. If you fit the SEC

---

[29] The SEC classifies a trader as a *pattern day trader* if the trader maintains less than $25,000 in a brokerage account and if that person buys and sells a security in the same trading day at least four times in a five-day period. Furthermore, those same-day trades must make up at least 6% of the trader's activity during that period. Pattern day traders are subject to special rules, one which results in your account being frozen for 90 days to prohibit such day trading activities.

description, you could find yourself locked out of establishing new positions (you can only close existing open positions) for ninety days. Although most traders need not be concerned with this regulation it is something to consider if you intend to trade frequently. If you are averaging in and out of positions resulting in entry and exit trades for the same stock in the same day, you could find yourself designated as a *pattern day trader.*

For the majority of traders, an effective account size revolves around what your objective is and what you have to work with. Make certain to set your monetary goals correctly when you start this endeavor so that you do not end up falling into the mental money traps outlined above. You can start with as little as $5000 or $10,000 if you have your priorities straight. With this amount of money, you can practice the risk mitigation strategies introduced in the following section. Once you are comfortable trading with a small amount of capital and you have developed a successful approach to trading, add more capital to your trading account and begin along the path to financial independence.

If your goal is to make money, then seriously consider an account size where (given a return of 15% a year), the money you make is worth the effort you put into the exercise. For some, this may be $35,000 while for others it may be more like $70,000 or even $100,000.

Risk Mitigation

Trading inherently involves the concept of future time, something necessarily unknown. As a result, each trade carries risk whether recognized or not. Risk is always present in trading, that's a given. The key, though, is to recognize it and take steps to minimize it.

The other aspect of risk is that **risk is not constant** ... **it is always changing**. There are times when the same position carries more risk than at other times. In fact, there are many times where your risk is a combination of multiple risk factors, not just one.

Risk, much like the market, ebbs and flows. So how do you deal with it? It turns out that in today's trading environment, there are many tools available to the *little guy* to not only minimize risk, but to turn it into an advantage to some degree.

Partial Buys and Sells

One of the most tried and true methods for dealing with all types of risk is to make partial buys and sells. If you are constantly scaling in and out of positions, you are reducing your risk by booking partial profits or incurring partial yet minimal losses. Since no one knows for sure how far a position will advance or decline a priori, a significant advantage to scaling in and out of positions is that you don't need to know something that is unknowable such as the future price of a position. Sure you are always seeking to *speculate* about what that may be since *speculation* is a key part of trading. When you create a thesis, you are *speculating*. When you purchase a stock, you are *speculating*. Speculating is inherent to trading and making partial buys and sells lets you reduce that error factor that is necessarily associated with speculating.

Scaling in and out of positions assumes that trades will, more often than not, move back and forth on their way to an eventual price point. As you know, the vast majority of trades do not go straight up or straight down, but instead tend to move back and forth as they work their way higher, lower or sideways over time. The fact that stocks move back and forth, is what lies at the heart of scaling in and out of positions.

As an example, let's say you purchase 100 shares of stock at $10 and it eventually trades to $12. One option is to buy it at $10, hold it until $12, and then sell it. Assuming that you are able to buy it at the low and sell it at the high, the result would be that you end up making $2 per share, or $200 on the entire transaction (excluding minor commission costs).

But what if you were to instead buy 100 shares at $10 and then sell 25 shares at $10.50. Now imagine that you repurchased those shares at $10.30 then turned around and made another partial sale at $11.00. Continuing on with this example, assume another repurchase of 25 shares at $10.75 and so forth as the stock gradually moves to $12. In this most optimistic case, you would make far more by buying on price weakness and selling on price strength as the stock ebbed and flowed higher. Naturally, the downside to doing this is, that at any point, the stock might not ebb back to allow you to repurchase those shares you sold at a lower price point. In that case you would end up with fewer shares once you reached the finish line of $12 per share and, depending on where that occurred, you may end up actually making less money – not more.

A key aspect to buying and selling the shares as they work higher and lower is that you are reducing other risk factors (overnight and exogenous risk being the more obvious) each time you make a sell. You have less exposure to the whims of the market until you repurchase those shares once more. This unforeseen benefit is not inconsequential. It also results in you having additional money for other purchases.

Realize that, for a long position, you buy on weakness and sell on strength *when you are in a winning trade.* You do not average down and purchase more when you are in a losing trade (unless you had originally planned to scale into the trade at lower prices). Scaling into a trade as the price moves against you is a very bad idea and an equally bad habit that eventually will lead to large losses and much angst. If your trading plan *originally* called for such a strategy, that is one thing; but if it didn't that's definitely another.

Dollar Cost Averaging

Partial buys and sells is **not** dollar cost averaging. If you were to survey the investing landscape, the vast majority of individual investors are of the *dollar cost averaging* type. This is the bill of goods that Wall Street has sold them for the past half century. The plan, as presented by Wall Street, is that you should deposit a set amount of money into your investment account on a monthly or quarterly basis. Those funds are used to immediately purchase equities (IRA and pension funds are the typical vehicles) without regard to the overall direction of the market. Wall Street, of course, suggests that you do so using mutual funds (surely it's not because of the fat fees they collect from you when selling you those funds), as they recite a myriad of stale and skewed facts to support this strategy.

One such myth is that the majority of the gains in the markets occur on just a few large up days in the market. The implication is that if you are not invested *all the time* then you will likely miss those bursts higher and consequently under perform the market over time. Of course they fail to tell you that if you had sidestepped the large move down that almost always precedes those large up moves, you would have probably been better off.

Another set of failure logic is that the market is random and cannot be timed. In fact, there was a famous book first published in 1973 titled <u>A Random Walk Down</u>

Wall Street[30] that purported, among other things that investors should buy and hold a broad set of instruments. In doing so, over time, they would perform as well or even better than professionals.

Although Wall Street initially disavowed the premise that a *monkey throwing darts at the Wall Street Journal* could outperform a professional money manager, they eventually spun the book to their advantage. They played up another premise of the book suggesting you should always be invested in the market – through thick and thin. Wall Street brokers love you to buy and never sell.

The concept of dollar cost averaging is fed by the above sort of logic. It suggests that if the market goes down, you are better off because you are buying more stock at cheaper prices. On the other, when the market goes up, you are doing the opposite (buying fewer shares at higher prices). Assuming that in the long run the market always increases, dollar cost averaging supposedly provides you with an *average* entry price that is superior to what you would have received had you tried to time the market. Clearly there are numerous implied assumptions here, many of which I cannot agree. After all, I am suggesting that you can reasonably time the market.

---

[30] Malkiel, Burton Gordon, <u>A Random Walk Down Wall Street,</u> 1973, W.W. Norton & Company Inc., 1973, ISBN-13:978-0-393-06245-8

Notice the assumption though, *the market trends higher over time*. Over the long run this is indeed true for two reasons:

1. Inflation is ever present and inflation implies that *everything* becomes more expensive over time – including stocks.
2. When Wall Street cites the *market,* they are referring to the major indexes. But how are those indexes constructed? It turns out that Wall Street constructs the indexes and constantly tweaks the indexes by removing weak stocks and replacing them with stronger ones. It is in this way that the overall value of the index continues to *increase over time* because the components of the index are cherry picked *all the time.*

Given the above, it is no wonder that investors look at their portfolio and wonder why they are not seeing the same increases in the value of their stocks as in the *market.* It's because they have not cherry picked their portfolio. In fact, Wall Street brokerages have told them to simply buy a diversified basket of stocks and bonds and the rest will take care of itself. It represents yet another example of a Wall Street ruse most have bought into.

Even with these factors though, there have been long stretches of time (on the order of decades) where the market has not moved higher. In fact, if you just look at recent history, there were people who purchased Cisco in 2000 at $70 or more. Cisco still trades at less than a third of this price 8 years later. These poor buy and hold "investors" may hold it for decades before it ever gets back to that initial purchase price. The same is true of a myriad of other stocks that are in the same situation. Wall Street says not to worry because you *really haven't lost money if you don't sell.* Nonsense! You have lost both the money and the opportunity costs for all those years you hold on.

To blindly assume you can put your money in the market on a regular basis and expect it to magically increase in value over time is unlikely to occur. Although dollar cost averaging can work given an astute stock purchasing strategy that complements the continued buying, the results are a lot more two-sided than those presented to the investing public. Here, just like elsewhere, your timing is critical. Attaining wealth from stock purchases is not a right everyone gets to exercise!

Partial buys and sells are a much more predictable way of *investing*. After some study, most anyone can understand what a trend is and that the market consists of trends. These trends themselves are comprised of multiple time frames. Why not simply remove some or all of your money and move to the safety of cash when the market becomes unpredictable? It's really not that hard to do. There are almost always plenty of technical warning signs in the charts providing early indications of near term problems. When most stocks stop moving higher, it's pretty clear that something is happening. Why not take some profits off the table, move to cash, and then re-invest larger amounts at cheaper prices rather than holding on as your stocks lose value as the market depreciates? What if the losing continues a lot longer than you think? What if it takes a decade? Are you going to dollar cost average for a decade? Are you really going to be better off?

Partial buys and sells are the way to increase portfolio performance, not the nonsense bill of goods that Wall Street sells called dollar cost averaging.

Mixing Long and Short Positions in a Portfolio

I have previously mentioned that another way to mitigate risk is to hold both long and short positions simultaneously in a portfolio. Simultaneously holding long and short positions works because the general market is strongly trending (either up or down) only about 30% of the time. The rest of the time, it is consolidating (going sideways) which implies that some stocks are moving higher while others are moving lower. If you can determine the general trend of the various sectors of the market, you can position yourself long in the stronger sectors while short in the weaker ones.

Historically, it was necessary to do this with buys and sells of individual stocks within the sectors identified as strong or weak. Unfortunately, individual stock buys and short sales do carry greater risk than buying and selling a large number of stocks in the same sector. Over the last few years, so many instruments have been introduced that allow you to take positions in differing sectors through the use of Exchange Traded Funds (ETF) and Notes (ETN)[31]. The field of ETF and ETN instruments is constantly changing as new ones are introduced and those that do not catch on are retired.

For example, recently introduced instruments allow a trader to short an index by buying an ETF or an ETN. This is significant to the *little guy* because many small traders are apt to manage their IRA accounts as part of their overall trading portfolio. Since IRA accounts cannot hold outright short positions, these new instruments allow you to skirt this rule. Other instruments recently introduced are 2:1 leveraged instruments where buying one share effectively acts as if you had purchased 2 shares because the ETF moves at twice the rate of the index that they track.

---

[31] An ETF is a security that tracks an index, a commodity, or a basket of assets like an index fund. It trades like a stock though, thus it experiences price changes throughout the day as it is bought and sold. These instruments are advantageous because you get the diversification of an index fund as well as the ability to short (without margin).. The expense ratio is also cheaper than a typical mutual fund.

As a trader, it is important to understand what instruments are available for you to trade and how they work. Your ability to effectively reduce risk without reducing profit potential by a corresponding amount is what you are always striving for. Having a firm grasp of the types of trading vehicles available to you is essential in this endeavor and this continues to change as new instruments are introduced and others withdrawn. Depending on where the economy is in the business cycle, there will be general market sectors that end up winners while others are losers. By spreading your risk using an ETF or ETN, you can effectively purchase some specific market sectors while simultaneously short selling others – effectively reducing individual stock risk while maintaining your ability to profit.

Carrying Many Small Positions Rather than a Few Large Ones

When trading individual stock positions, spreading your risk across many trades rather than concentrating your entire portfolio into just a few is yet another way to reduce risk. Trading is a game of probabilities no matter what anyone wants to tell you. This is true whether you are trading based on fundamental or technical analysis. In any game of probability, there are winning and losing streaks. Winning streaks are easy to deal with as they pad your bank account. Losing streaks are what can be concerning because they have the possibility of depleting your capital base to a point where you can no longer trade. Spreading your risk is one way to mitigate that possibility.

Probably the most common risk adverse strategy is to spread risk out over multiple trades. Why would you want to spread risk over a large number of trades? Clearly not all trades will rise together, but the converse is also true; not all of them fall at the same time either. So why not press for larger returns by concentrating your holdings in one or two stocks? The easy answer is provided by the old proverb, "Don't put all your eggs in one basket." If you concentrate all your efforts into two stocks and both stocks end up losers, how much is your portfolio affected?

So how many differing positions should you attempt to maintain? If you have roughly $100,000 in trading capital and are purchasing and maintaining some fifty stocks with an average $2000 invested in each of the fifty stocks, would this be ideal? The answer is "probably yes, as long as you can manage that many positions effectively". The ability to manage a large number of positions is easier than you expect. If you create a portfolio through your brokerage firm or any of the many freely available portfolio management sites on the Internet, sort the positions you hold by the percentage change in price. On a day-to-day basis, the positions that you care about are those that are moving up or down by a large percentage. In this way, you can safely ignore the majority of the positions you hold most days while concentrating only on those at the fringes. It's effective and, more importantly, it enables you to effectively mitigate risk by spreading that risk across many simultaneous trades. It makes for a winning strategy.

Positions in Multiple Non-correlated Sectors

Earlier I touched on another effective method for mitigating your risks while trading. The idea of holding positions in non-correlated sectors (see the section on *Asset Class Risk*). As discussed, holding many positions open simultaneously provides you with some degree of risk mitigation as long as they holdings are not highly correlated? If they are correlated, that does nothing to reduce your risk. To reduce your risk, take a larger view of the stocks you are trading, the sectors that they trade in, and the relationship between the sectors. Only then will you actually achieve your goal and only then will you really achieve a real reduction in risk.

One last note on diversification though – it shouldn't be treated as a panacea. If you truly want to be fully diversified, you should simply purchase a broad based index like the S&P 500 and forget trying to play an edge with your chart reading abilities. Instead you would simply buy the S&P 500 and achieve your diversification easily. But, as a trader, the whole point of trading is to outperform the indexes. Therefore although diversification is justified to some degree, too much of a good thing can have bad consequences.

Spreading Risk across Borders

Another development that greatly aids the *little guy* in risk management (if used appropriately) are American Depository Receipts (ADR) and ETF products specifically designed to let you trade in the global markets. Historically, the small trader was limited to the purchase or sale of a small group of ADR issues that traded on U.S. exchanges. These ADR certificates are issued by U.S. banks and represent a specific number of shares of a foreign stock traded on a U.S. stock exchange. In other words, they trade just like any other stock. Nowadays, with the advent of ETF products, there are specific products that target foreign indexes[32].

By purchasing or short selling an ETF that mimics a foreign market exchange, you spread your risk across borders at a cost that is no different than buying or selling a stock on a local exchange. How could you use these instruments to reduce risk? Well, there are several ways. Here is an example.

---

[32] ETFConnect.com is a great place to bookmark and visit from time to time as they list all the products available and new ones coming out in the ETF and ETN world.

The simplest and most straightforward approach would be to spread your risk from owning just American companies to include foreign companies. If you are bullish on equity markets and semi-conductor stocks in general, with a little research you would find that Taiwan is home to an abundance of semi-conductor stocks. As a result, you could spread your risk from buying just American semi-conductor stocks to include Taiwanese semi-conductor stocks as well. You do this by either by purchasing the EWT ETF[33] or maybe one or more Taiwanese semi-conductor s ADR stocks such as Taiwan Semiconductor (TSM).

The downside risk in trading across borders is that of currency fluctuations. Foreign companies can easily be affected by exchange rates between the U.S. and the foreign countries. If you choose to spread risk in this manner, have some understanding of the currency risks that are applicable because, like most things in finance, they can work either for or against you.

Spreading risk across borders has its place but, like all other trades, there are some advantages and disadvantages. There are times when it makes sense to do so and times where it doesn't. Risk mitigation has its place and its time. Risks are forever changing. Your job is to recognize both what works and when it works,

---

[33] EWT is the symbol for the Taiwanese market which has a heavy overall weighting of semi-conductor stocks in it.

then to use your findings to seek reduced risk. If you are unsure about a risk mitigation strategy, then don't employ it as it is likely to complicate matters.

Cash

One of the simplest yet most effective risk mitigation strategies available to the *little guy* is the relative ease and small cost of moving to cash when circumstances dictate. It's not sexy, and seldom advertised, but it offers a huge advantage to a small trader.

Unlike a casino where you have to decide to play a hand before you see your cards, in the virtual casinos of Wall Street, you are able to see your hand before you decide to play. Naturally, if the hand looks really good, then you want to play with more money, not less. Conversely, if it looks bad, you either want to play with less money or skip that hand altogether and wait for a subsequent game. As a small trader, you simply are unlikely to have any kind of effect on the liquidity of the market (no matter how small the market is for the stocks you are liquidating) so there's no additional cost associated with moving to cash (other than the minimal transaction cost). There are opportunity costs but those costs cut both ways.

Cash is an asset. It is a safe asset. Cash is your friend – it can only cost you from an opportunity cost standpoint but can easily save you a bundle of money though.

When your money is in the market, it is at risk. When the risk becomes too great and uncertainty increases, moving all or some of that risk out of your portfolio and into cash is a good thing. As a trading strategy, Cashing out, is a good practice, particularly during uncertain market times.

Predefining Risks and Protecting with Stops

The final and highly effective strategy in mitigating risks is to make certain that you identify your risks *prior* to entering the trade. Buying or selling short without a predefined exit point (for both the successful and unsuccessful result to the trade) is a trading sin. Without a predefined stop, you are guaranteeing that, over time, you will likely suffer huge draw downs and potentially lose a large portion of your trading capital. Falling into this trading trap is unfathomable for both a large or small trader, but particularly the small trader since a large loss of capital can be completely debilitating to future trading.

There are many who suggest that to predefine risk is fine but predefining reward is short-sighted. In particular, trend traders tend to look upon this process as limiting your profit potential. The problem with not defining your potential reward is that without a reward target, how can you make a decision about whether the potential reward sufficiently outweighs the potential risk prior to entering into a trade?

Calculating Risk/Reward Ratios

If there is a cornerstone to any trading philosophy, it starts with the risk versus reward calculation. Although identifying good risk-to-reward trades does not guarantee success, the converse almost always guarantees failure. Contrary to popular thought, there are many successful traders that use many successful and contradicting trading styles. If you were to ask them whether they consider the risk to the reward with respect to each trade they expect to make, they would answer in the affirmative. Successful conservative and speculative traders alike all view their trades in terms of the risk they are taking juxtaposed to the reward they expect to receive. If the risk doesn't outweigh the reward by some amount (it differs from one trader to the next), then they walk away from the trade.

So what do I mean by a good risk-to-reward trade? As I have implicitly indicated already in earlier sections of this book, what you are looking for in a trade is to identify what your expected exit price will be once you enter the trade (on both the winning and losing side). Before you make the trade, you need some concrete idea as to the potential losses as compared to the potential gains. This is the concept behind the risk (losses) to reward (gains) paradigm.

To implement this paradigm, technical traders do the following:

1. Look for chart patterns that exhibit a greater than 50/50 chance of repeating themselves over and over again.
2. Attempt to recognize those patterns in current charts.
3. Identify potential entry and exit points. Entry and exit points are typically associated with support and resistance areas of the charts[34].

To properly calculate the risk-to-reward of a trade, identify three criteria; the entry point; the exit point; and the probability that the trade will succeed. The latter is not easy to do with any degree of reliability until you have some historical data and experience to work with. An example should help to crystallize the thought.

As a technical trader, classify your trades based on the patterns you are trading. You should keep a record of each trade you make, noting the essential details of the trade so you can later analyze what does and doesn't work. With historical data, analyze your performance and continue to improve your trading (see the section

---

[34] Chart support and resistance can be determined in many different ways such as moving averages and trend lines. For further information, refer to one of the many books on technical trading.

Trade Data - your Trading Diary for more extensive coverage). Record the details you have when you open the trade and again once the trade is closed. This gives you a simple log of each trade you make. Place these trade histories in either a database or spreadsheet. When first experimenting with trading records, one should error on the side of simplicity. Having too many factors is no better than having none at all. Here's a very simple spreadsheet entry (see Table 5) for the chart that follows (Figure 11).

Table 5 - Simple Trade Data Recording

Symbol	Entry	Type	Shares	Stop	Target	Pattern
NEM	$28.79	Short	100	$30.28	$25.33	Gap

Figure 11 - Newmont Mining - May, 2002

The risk-to-reward data entry in Table 5 represents the simplest form of a trading record you can create. It provides the essential data associated with your trade yet provides you with historical data you can later analyze to improve your trading. It includes the following:

Symbol	The stock you are trading.
Entry	Your entry price.
Type	Whether the trade was a long or a short sell.
Shares	How many shares you bought or sold short.
Stop	The price point where you expect to exit if

	your analysis proves wrong. For a short sell, the stop price is above the entry price. For a long purchase, the stop is lower.
Target	The price target where you expect to exit the stock if your analysis proved correct.
Pattern	The reason you made the trade. As a technical trader, you are going to have five or ten technical patterns that you are looking for that you end up trading over and over again. If you are a fundamental trader, there are going to be five or ten primary reasons for entering the trade like the PE and maybe management of the company. Whatever your reason, note it and do so consistently for each trade taken.

Recognize that once you have entered the data into your spreadsheet, let it be final. Many times there is the desire to tweak the numbers a bit to *make them work*.

When people tend to get attached to their ideas and/or stocks their desire to make a trade in that stock is great. As a result, they alter their risk-to-reward data so that the trade makes sense. In the chart above, you may go back and change the target exit price to $24 even though the support lies just above $25 in order to *justify* the trade, but the trader inside you knows that the numbers are what they are. Changing them in your spreadsheet is not going to change reality. You are only fooling yourself and putting your money at greater risk. Avoid such temptations.

It may help you to follow this simple procedure when evaluating a potential trade:

1. Always determine your support and resistance areas **first** on the charts. Once identified, allow sufficient overshoot and undershoot of prices as well[35]. Put those numbers into your spreadsheet as the stop loss and target price points.
2. Plug in the entry price and ask yourself "Does the risk-to-reward make sense?"
3. If the risk-to-reward doesn't make sense, change the entry price – **not the stop or target prices**! Only tinker with the entry price because the support and resistance points are set in stone by the chart. You can't change them because they are what they are. You can only change where you enter the trade. Where you enter the trade defines whether the risk-to-reward ratio makes for a profitable trade setup. If it doesn't work out, don't sweat it because there's always another trade.

---

[35] Stock prices, more often than not, either overshoot or undershoot the resistance and support areas on a chart. Thus, you have to allow some leeway when placing your stops and when considering your exit point on winning trades. The closer you set your stop to the target stop price, the greater the likelihood that you will in fact stop out. The art of trading is leaving enough room but not too much so that when you are stopped out you are indeed actually wrong and the stop *saves you* from larger losses. Same is true of the exit on a profitable trade. You want to get as much as possible, but not get greedy and miss the exit altogether.

Once you begin to keep records of your trading history, some small additions to the data you are recording may prove useful. For example, you can have your spreadsheet or database software automatically compute your loss risk and profit potential[36] from the target and stop price data. Another simple, yet automatic computation is the risk-to-reward ratio. Here's the enhanced record with these additions.

Table 6 - Embellished Trading Record

Symbol	Entry	Type	Shares	Stop	Target	Pattern
NEM	$28.79	Short	100	$30.28	$25.33	Gap

R/R Ratio[37]	Loss Risk	Profit Potential
2.3	-$149.00	$346.00

---

[36] The loss risk is the difference between the entry and (stop) exit prices times the number of shares traded. The profit potential is the same formula where the exit is the target price rather than the stop price.

[37] The risk to reward calculation is (Stop Price – Entry Price) / (Entry Price – Target Price).

Ranking Trades and the Spreadsheet

A problem that every trader faces on a day-to-day basis is the question; "Is this trader better than that one?" where better is defined as a combination of:

1. Expected reward
2. Expected risk
3. Confidence in the expected risk and reward (probability of success)
4. The expected time interval needed to complete the trade (time from entry to exit)

Over time you realize that there are many more ideas than there is money, and being able to discern where you do and don't put your money is as big a job as any. Expected reward and risk are fairly straightforward; you look on a chart for resistance and support and, given your time frame for the trade, you estimate exit price points for both the successful and unsuccessful results for the trade. The following paragraphs examine the other two factors in more detail.

Trade Length

The length of time that you are in a trade is important to the risk-to-reward calculations. Like a store that is always seeking to turn over its inventory as fast as possible, a trader should be looking to do something along the same lines. You want that capital exposed to winning trades – winning trades that are initiated and closed sooner rather than later. If the same returns generated from a trade that takes two weeks versus one that takes two months, which trade is better? Clearly the one that only took two weeks is better. All things being equal, the shorter the trade length, the better your returns are going to be (assuming you are a successful trader). Given this, you may already be wondering how you can estimate if a trade is likely to take a long time versus a short period of time.

The primary input to trade length determination is a familiarity with the stock you are trading and the type of market environment you are trading in. Being familiar with a particular stock means that you have a sense of what the typical price spread[38] is for the stock on a daily basis as well as an average price spread on a weekly basis. You can do this programmatically if you have open/high/low/close data available to you on a daily basis. There are a number of service providers who provide a beta[39] measure, which is another way of

---

[38] Price spread is the difference between the high and the low on a given day or, in this case, the difference between the low yesterday and the high today (the opposite if you are short selling the stock).

[39] Beta is defined as a risk measure comparing the volatility of a stock's price movement to the general market. A beta of 1 implies that the stock has the same volatility as the general market where a beta of 1.25 would mean it is likely to move 25% more than the general market over time.

comparing a stock's volatility (price spread) to all other stocks. Stocks that carry high beta values are likely to be in and out of your portfolio faster than stocks with low beta values. This is true since the more volatile stocks will either hit your stop or your target price sooner than less volatile ones.

The downside of trading a volatile stock is just that, the volatility. When trading a volatile stock, scale down the size (how many shares you buy or sell) and give some extra room to your stop loss. You also have to take partial profits (if not all profits) at your target prices because in a volatile stock, "What's there today may be gone tomorrow."

Probability of Success

The probability of success in any trade is a somewhat arbitrary assessment unless you have historical data. Once you have data, you can analyze your potential for success. Taking the previously presented simple spreadsheet entry, there are at least three ways you can analyze the success probability of a potential trade based on your past trading data. Here's the table entry again for convenience.

Table 7 - Embellished Trading Record (reprinted)

Symbol	Entry	Type	Shares	Stop	Target	Pattern
NEM	$28.79	Short	100	$30.28	$25.33	Gap

R/R Ratio[40]	Loss Risk	Profit Potential
2.3	-$149.00	$346.00

Once you have 50 or 100 trades to analyze, you might want to look at all trades that exhibited the same pattern as the one you are now considering (in this case a gap pattern). Of those previous trades, how many were successful and how many failed? How many of them were short sell trades versus long purchases? How many trades with a risk reward of 2.3 or less were successful? How about between 3 or 4? How about over 5?

The answers to these types of questions will yield some insight to how probable a success is in this kind of trade. If you find that the success ratio is less than 60% for all of the above questions, then you should spend some time analyzing how you made those trades. It may require you to look at how other traders successfully

---

[40] The risk to reward calculation is (Stop Price – Entry Price) / (Entry Price – Target Price).

use that type of trading pattern. It could be that you are too impatient and make the purchase prematurely or that there is a variation to the trade setup for this pattern that performs better. Whatever the case, if you are not achieving a success rate of 60% or better for a given trading pattern, then you either need to determine why or quit trading that type of pattern.

Over time you will most likely decide that there are some other data points that may be worth analyzing (like the general trend of the sector that a stock trades in and/or the general trend of the exchange this stock trades on). Whatever you can hypothesize as having a potential significant influence for the success or failure of your trade can be entered into your trading history and analyzed for clues as to how you can improve. Personally, I have recorded over five years worth of data at this point and continue to do so each day I trade. It only takes a few minutes of your time but is worth a small fortune over time once analyzed.

Historical trading data is the fundamental basis of all potential trade ranking systems. The ambitious traders attempt to construct a confidence factor that they associate with their potential trades. The confidence factor itself is typically based on several factors. They might include things like the probability that the technical pattern is favorable; the probability of the market contributing to your individual stock's success; the beta of the stock; and how far away you place your *stop loss order* in relation to the entry price and the stock's volatility. Regardless of the factors you experiment with, it is important that you keep your data available for study over time so that you can continue to refine your system. Without periodic scrutiny, your ranking system can loose its value overtime as the markets are dynamic and always changing. Don't be afraid to adapt slightly over time to capture the changing dynamics of the market.

Risk Adverse Trading Strategy

Putting together a trading strategy implies that you have a clear cut objective, a concisely stated goal. Given that your goal should be to become a successful trader – a person who buys and sells financials instruments and **consistently produces above average** short-term profits – then it is an encumbrance upon you to come up with a plan that enables you to meet that goal. You need a plan that is not abstract, but instead concrete and able to easily implement. The plan needs to be simple and concise, yet complete enough to keep you on the correct path to successful trading. Such a plan is possible. It's one that I use in my day-to-day trading activities. Simply stated, to achieve above average short-term profits on a consistent basis, focus on **keeping your portfolio at or near the highs.** An action plan for doing that is embodied in the following statement:

To achieve your goals of successful trading, focus on keeping your portfolio value within a few percentage points of your all time highs and regularly achieving new highs throughout the trading year.

This is a concrete, actionable statement – a plan that allows you to achieve the theoretical definition of a successful trader. By staying within a *few percentage points of your all time high,* I am suggesting that you should **always** do your best to stay within 5% of the highs. By saying that you are *regularly making new highs,* I am implying that every three or four months (at a minimum) you should be making new highs in your overall portfolio value.

If you do the above, you are accomplishing a lot of individual items that are necessarily implementing a risk adverse trading strategy that is also profit rich. What flows from such a strategy is a set of activities that, when taken as a whole, push you towards your goal of being a successful trader.

Now you have a goal that you can use to drive your day-to-day activities. It is concrete and though not a necessary and sufficient condition for being a successful trader, it makes that achievement highly probable. So, how do you do this? It's done through Active Portfolio Management – a key concept discussed in the next chapter.

Chapter

9

Active Portfolio Management

T here are many strategies that one can use to successfully trade. A trading strategy of trend trading (made famous by Richard Dennis and later in the Turtle Trading group[41]) is unquestionably successful, but so is the opposite style sometimes referred to as fade trading[42]. In between these to extremes is a hodge-podge of competing strategies utilizing untold numbers of supposedly predictive tools and methodologies that promise to lead one on the path to successful trading. In the end though, trading boils

---

[41] Faith Curtis, <u>Way of the Turtle: The Secret Methods that Turned Ordinary People into Legendary Traders</u>, McGraw-Hill, 2007, ISBN-13: 978-0-07-148664-4.

[42] Fade trading is essentially the strategy of trading against the prevailing short-term trends yet also trading with the intermediate or long-term trend.

down to the individual; to experimentation and to a methodical and sometimes frustrating trial-by-error method of finding one's own way. Because trading is an individual experience and the fact that not all individuals are the same, trading is in many ways different for everyone. What is successful for George Soros[43] may not necessarily be successful for you.

Active portfolio management is a term I've coined to get across the idea that portfolio management is not a passive endeavor. The success or failure of the *little guy* is influenced most significantly by the ability or inability to actively manage your own portfolio. Again, before I try and talk about how to do this, I must first define what it is.

> Portfolio Management - The art and science of making decisions about investment mix and policy, matching investments to objectives, making asset allocation for individuals and institutions, and balancing risk vs. performance.[44]

By adding *active* to this definition and narrowing it to pertain to the small trader, you get a better sense of my thought process. *Active portfolio management* is

---

[43] Soros George, The Alchemy of Finance, John Wiley & Sons Inc., 1987. ISBN 0-471-04343-3

[44] "Portfolio management." *Investopedia.com*. Investopedia Inc. 08 Apr. 2007. <Dictionary.com http://dictionary.reference.com/browse/portfolio management>.

Active Portfolio Management - The art and science of **active engagement** in the decision making progress regarding investment mix and policy for the small trader; balancing risk vs. performance.

Active engagement in this process is what separates the average traders from the outstanding ones. Regardless of the trading strategies employed, active portfolio management is what truly separates the successful traders from all the rest.

Active portfolio management is the active engagement in all the ideas presented in the preceding chapters with respect to your portfolio. The best way to explain it, is to do it. The remainder of this chapter sets out to do just that. Let me walk through the steps of how I first form a trading thesis with regards to the market followed by sector analysis, and then work lower to the actual trades. I'll set up two trades; first walking through the preparation for entry, the actual execution and then the active management of the trades. Finally, I'll end it all with the closing of the trades.

Learning by example is an excellent way to more fully grasp a concept. In doing so, this exercise will elucidate the act of **keeping your portfolio at the highs** so that the ideas embodied are understood as both achievable and worthwhile.

Trade Preparation – Turning a Thesis into an Action Plan

Active portfolio management is the idea of actively managing your positions within the larger context of your overall thesis (bias) towards the markets. For example, as I write this section of the book in the spring of 2008, the general equity market appears to be in a large consolidation range with a lot of uncertainty. Inflation is running rampant (although the government consistently understates it in their CPI and PPI reports) while the dollar has depreciated significantly over the past few months and the past few years. Commodities are all the rage as is anything related to them. Basic materials, agriculture, and energy have been the leading market sectors for months while most other sectors have been punished most of this year. The average share price has declined significantly, although if you

---

[45] The GG trade was added as a paired trade to the FXE trade (see the remainder of the chapter for details) in order to display some of the risk minimization principles and the concept of hedged trading. My actual trades at the time involved the shorting of the FXE while maintaining a mixture of long positions in gold stocks, not just GG.

look at the broad indexes, it doesn't seem that bad (this is a somewhat misleading statistic because the primary averages such as the S&P 500 and the NASDAQ are weighted averages, where a few large and strong stocks can mask the weakness of the majority). Financials, in particular, have been the weakest sector.

Here are a few charts that visibly demonstrate how this general thesis is currently playing out in the markets. Consider first the idea that the general equity markets are in a large consolidation range. Figure 12 is a one-year chart of the S&P 500.

Note: The large price range that the S&P 500 is trading at from roughly 1275 SPX to 1400 as annotated on the chart.

Figure 12 - S&P 500 - April 2008

Regarding this trading range, one of the first issues you must contend with in any market is to decide what the current market cycle is (as described previously in the section on the *Cyclicality of the Markets*). As illustrated above, the market has recently undergone a large correction that produced increased volume on the way down. Since then, volume has decreased and prices have begun to work their way higher. The best guess of the current market phase is that it is either still in the mark-down phase or potentially in the early stages of the accumulation phase. A visual picture of the short, intermediate, and long-term trend of the S&P 500 is illustrated in Figure 13.

154

Figure 13 – S&P 500 Market Price Trend Cube

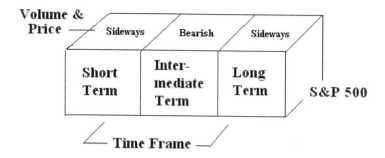

Staying with the big picture, inflation has significantly increased over the past year although you wouldn't know that by the government statistics that are being reported. An alternate set of statistics published by John Williams[46] explains that in the early 1990's, the CPI statistics were changed and tied to the cost of living increases. Soon afterwards, they began to be under reported since lower CPI data meant lower cost of living increases that the government has to pay. Those misleading statistics are now taken for granted. Figure 14 shows what John Williams considers to be the actual Consumer Price Index. By his calculations, inflation is currently running at a 12% clip.

---

[46] John Williams, <u>Shadow Government Statistics</u>, http://www.shadowstats.com, Spring of 2008.

Figure 14 - True CPI Statistics

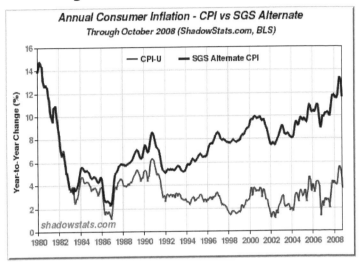

Annual Consumer Inflation - CPI vs SGS Alternate
Through October 2008 (ShadowStats.com, BLS)

Looking elsewhere, this picture of inflation manifests itself most everywhere. The USO (United States Oil) ETF, which is a proxy for the price of oil (West Texas Intermediate Crude), shows that this basic commodity has ascended without any serious consolidation in price for the past year (see Figure 15).

Figure 15 - USO (United States Oil ETF)

Inflation tends to be felt most acutely when the currency of the country experiencing the inflation loses its value. Figure 16 shows the uninterrupted decline of the dollar. Though it has been trying to grope for a bottom over the past month (as shown on the chart), it has yet to find one.

Figure 16 - Dollar Index

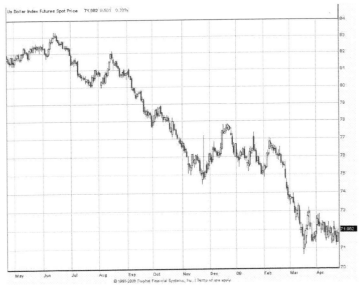

Although these few charts represent only a partial picture of the entire market, they do provide a reasonable broad brush stroke view of the current environment. Depending on what type of trader you are[47], you can easily begin to identify some trades to make given these broad brush strokes I have just provided. Using the risk-to-reward formula, you could

---

[47] As an example, a fade trader would be searching for opportunities to purchase stocks in the strong sectors on a retrace in price or even short the weaker sectors on this recent price strength. The momentum trader would, on the other hand, look for an opportunity to get aboard these hot sectors on the next breakout move higher.

158

look at buying an instrument that mimics the dollar index or maybe short sell the broad S&P 500 via the SPY[48] or some other instrument. It all depends on your time frame and trading bias. The likelihood of success for each of these potential trades reduces to this question: "At what price points will this instrument likely trade at during the time frame you trade it?"

How you decide to trade the market greatly depends on how you answer that question. In fact, you might look at the S&P 500 chart and decide it is too uncertain at this point in time and that you don't want to trade the SPY ETF given the trends and current price. Rather than force a trade in a situation where the uncertainty and volatility are too great, you could instead focus your trade search elsewhere. And where might you focus in this time frame if not the general equity markets? Well that requires a review of the broad sectors to identify other potential opportunities.

Considering the devaluation of the dollar and the rise in oil prices, you can see that the prices associated with these markets have extended far beyond what is normally expected for the time frame being considered. When you see that something has moved way beyond what is expected, that should alert you to the possibility

---

[48] SPY is the trading symbol for the SPDR TRUST SR 1 ETF which trades on the AMEX. It essentially is a proxy for the broad basket of stocks known as the S&P 500.

of opportunity. That leads us to look at other sectors in this broad space; other commodities besides oil that might present opportunity.

For example, you may ask yourself, what are the agricultural related stocks doing? Figure 17 is a reasonable representation of how the basic grain commodities are performing. DBA is an ETF that has an equal weighting of corn, soybeans, wheat, and sugar. For example, look at how it has begun to fall relative to the chart of oil. Is it possibly a harbinger of lower commodity prices or is it just taking a breather before heading higher once more?

Figure 17 - DBA (Deutsche Bank Agricultural Fund)

As annotated on the chart, you can see that the DBA ETF is way off its highest price and is instead trading in the middle of a four-plus point range (a 10% range). What about other commodities? How about precious metals like gold?

Figure 18 - GLD (StreetTRACKS Gold Shares ETF)

Interestingly, the GLD ETF is exhibiting the same weakness as seen in the DBA chart. Given this glance across the markets, you can begin to come to some conclusions: The weak dollar has been the driving force for the rise in all commodities, but some of them are losing steam. This is happening in concert with the dollar firming. The one commodity that remains in a stubborn uptrend is the oil market. One opportunity might be to consider shorting oil or oil related equities but that would be very risky since it hasn't shown any indication of failing yet. Excessive risk is what you are trying to avoid!

Another thought is that since the grains and the precious metals are exhibiting weakness, you could conclude that there is a good chance that the dollar strength may not be fleeting. That would offer an opportunity to short sell one of the currency ETF instruments. As you can see from Figure 19, the EURO ETF (The Euro currency proxy), unlike grains, metals, and the dollar, has not began to sell off in any meaningful way. It should though, and that represents an opportunity.

Figure 19 - EURO ETF

When you are preparing for a trade, the above thoughts represent the logical steps you should follow. To do this, look at the large picture and consider the broad trading landscape. Usually there are some sectors and stocks that are extended either on the way up or the way down. What you have to do is put together a picture of the market for yourself. This logical walkthrough is a practical application of establishing a thesis (see *Establishing a Market Thesis – a Trading Bias*).

Once you have formed a reasonable picture of the current market environment, this becomes your general thesis and your trades need to revolve around that thesis. As events unfold, you can either confirm the thesis or modify it as needed.

In summary, my broad current thesis for the short term trend time frame is that the equity markets are likely contained in a trading range; that the dollar is no longer falling, and that there is a divergence in price action between the Euro and most commodities versus the dollar.

Seeking Low Risk, High Reward Trades

Once you have a general thesis and have identified one or two aberrations in the market, your next task is to find some low risk, high reward trade setups. In the chapter on Trade Idea Generation, there was a discussion about stock scanners and how to use them. Having done your homework, you should have built and maintained a watch list of potential trades (both long and short) that you can now use to identify potential trades that are congruent with your trading thesis. You can also run some new screens that identify stocks in one or more sectors of the market that appear opportunistic.

Given that I am entertaining the thought of selling short the Euro because all commodities (with the exception of oil) have already sold off, it is reasonably logical to consider a good paired trade to go with it. A purchase of a solid gold stock – one that has already depreciated in price yet is in a strong long term bullish trend might be a good choice. Executing a screen search for the gold sector using the *bullish retrace scan* example shown on page 77, yields a number of potential stocks, one of which is Goldcorp Corporation.

Goldcorp Corporation is a gold stock that has sold off quite a bit already and would make a good paired trade with a short sell on the Euro. Since the precious metal (gold) is currently highly correlated with the Euro[49], a paired trade with these two instruments is both congruent with the general thesis and has less risk than a single direction trade. Since our thesis has the general market environment as trading sideways, trading a long and a short position simultaneously offers a profitable alternative that is in keeping with your desire to

---

[49] When the Euro rises, gold typically rises and vice versa.

maintain low risk (if needed, review *Mixing Long and Short Positions in a Portfolio* as a refresher as to why you might want to trade this way). If initiated properly, both sides of the trade should perform while protecting against both exogenous and overnight risks. In trader terminology, this is a form of a hedge trade.

> **Note:** The workability of this trade depends on you finding a solid gold stock that has retraced sufficiently to a good support area. If it all works out as planned, the gold stock should go sideways to higher while the Euro shares trade sideways to lower over the short-term time frame (anything from a few weeks to a few months).

Goldcorp (GG) – A Long Trade Setup

Here are three charts of Goldcorp (GG is the symbol), a gold stock that trades in the precious metals sector. This sector is a strong sector that is currently witnessing a general pull back. Within the sector, GG has pulled back a reasonable percentage already. The only difference between the three charts is the time frame. The first chart is for a 10-week time frame.

166

Figure 20 - Goldcorp - Short Term Trend

In this chart (see Figure 20), GG looks to be in a trading range. At the current price of $41.56, would this be a good point to make a purchase? The stock made a high just over $46, then retraced almost $10 back to just above $36 and now seems to be working its way higher again.

To determine whether buying this stock now might make sense, here's a chart with a longer time horizon – a two-year time frame (see Figure 21).

Figure 21 - Goldcorp - Intermediate Term Trend

With this chart, you get a little more context to make the potential buy decision. The trend over a longer period of time (last 9 months) has been up, resulting in much higher prices. Before that, however, the trend was generally down for the preceding year.

When looking at the longer term time frame, the type of risk you would have to take becomes clearer. A purchase at the present price ($41.56) with a stop under the $36 area could limit your risks, but that doesn't provide a very good risk-to-reward scenario because the most you can expect on the upside is a retest of the highs initially ($46.28). Another alternative would be to bring your stop closer (say $38.91 or so ... just under the recent lows), but as can be imagined, the risk of failure is reasonably high if that's how close the stop loss order is placed.

When you are considering a trade, you have to consider realistic risk first – where is the most realistic place to stop out for a loss on the trade yet provide every opportunity for the trade to succeed? This is the heart of your entry analysis – creating a risk-to-reward calculation before entering the position that contains the most realistic set of data points for the time frame being considered.

Looking at the chart of GG in Figure 21 and trying to be realistic about where a reasonable stop placement would be, it appears that the $30 area would be best. Placing the stop at that price point would provide the greatest opportunity for the trade to result in a success, without being stopped out for a loss.

If you assume that you would take at least partial profits (if not all profits) on a retest of the highs at $46 (which is the goal of the trade), then you can work the risk-to-reward calculation backwards to determine your potential entry point. You need at least a 2:1 reward to risk and your stop placement is at \$30. With a profit target at \$46, your entry needs to be \$35.33[50].

Looking at just this time frame though, it is still hard to know if an entry price of \$35.33 is a realistic entry point for this trade because prior to the last nine months, GG traded lower for the preceding 13 months. In fact, this two-year chart even has the look of a large sideways looking range bound market as well. If that is true, then a trade back to \$30 is not as unlikely as you would imagine. If the trend is higher and if this is just a normal retracing move off the highs, then \$30 is probably a good place to stop out if wrong.

Pulling the chart back even further (see Figure 22 for a four year chart), a clearer picture develops. Over this longer term time frame, the trend has definitely been higher for the majority of the four years. The current pull back in price (when viewed in the context of the very long-term trend), is probably just that – a pull back within the context of a continuing longer term up trend.

---

[50] For a long position, the formula is [Target Price – Entry Price = 2 * (Entry Price – Stop Price)]. The result of the math is \$35.33.

Figure 22 - Goldcorp - Long Term Trend

With this kind of information, the confidence in buying this stock with a larger stop loss order makes the most sense when combining the trade with a short sell on the Euro (see the next section). The paired trade, as viewed so far, appears to be a profitable setup.

Euro to Dollar (FXE) – A Short Trade Setup

The other half of the paired trade is a short sell on the FXE. Figure 19 displayed a one-year chart of the FXE. Figure 23 is that same chart displaying only 3 months of data to show more clearly what has developed recently. Note that in March, when the highs were hit, a

171

fairly high volume amount of selling set in (note the volume bars at the bottom of the chart).

Figure 23 - FXE - 3 Months View

The chart above has the appearance of being technically vulnerable to a further pull back. As indicated earlier, on the fundamental side, events are occurring that suggest the dollar should hold steady, if not continue to strengthen near term. For example, the Federal Reserve has been lowering the interest rates and has done so aggressively. This lowering of rates is what has pushed the dollar lower. Now the Federal Reserve is signaling (through speeches and comments) that it may be finished with lowering rates for a while. Add to that the fact that the European economies have yet to show a significant slowdown but are just starting to show signs of lower growth. As Europe slows, there will be perceived pressure on the ECB (The European equivalent of the Federal Reserve) to lower their rates. All of this points to a possible rebound in the dollar. If that happens, the Euro will subsequently trade lower. If nothing else, some sort of sideways to lower price range appears to be in the cards near term.

Calculating the Trade Mix

Once you have the trades identified (which implies that the risk-to-reward calculations are favorable), the next set of questions become apparent.

- Of all the potential trades identified, which ones are the best trades and in what time frame?
- How much should you trade?
- Do you purchase/sell all the shares at once or in increments over time?
- What is the best trade mix among all the potential trades?

In the real world, you would most likely have many more trade possibilities than just the two I have highlighted so far. The last bullet above is concerned with the notion of how to best spread your risk via the trade possibilities available to you. In this example, I've already done that for you by selecting two stocks to create a hedge trade (which is constructed to spread your risk). Many times, in a general market that is moving sideways, a spread trade is a superior alternative to a portfolio that is strictly long or short. It offers greater risk protection while simultaneously exploiting the likelihood that both trades can produce profits even though one is short and one is long.

The remaining questions scattered over the next few pages are questions that you should answer **before you make the trade**. These are the same questions that you must answer in order to actively manage your transactions and your portfolio. These questions are every bit as important as the actual identification of the trade itself. In fact, by answering these questions beforehand, you are putting your management roadmap into place prior to engaging in the trade. This almost always results in an increase in your trade success rate.

Determining the Best Trade and Trade Mix

Up until now, the only criterion used to determine if a trade was worthwhile was to calculate a risk versus reward for the potential trade. For the two trades being considered, a quick risk-to-reward calculation shows a 1:2.5 risk-to-reward on the FXE trade (if it was sold short at the current levels).

Table 8 - FXE Short Trade - Risk-to-Reward Calculation

Symbol	Entry	Type	Shares	Stop	Target
FXE	$157.92	Short	100	$160.21	$152.21

R/R Ratio	Loss Risk	Profit Potential	Pattern
1 to 2.5	-$229.00	$571.00	Resistance

The GG trades exhibits a 1:2 risk-to-reward as shown below and previously calculated.

Table 9 - GG Long Trade - Risk-to-Reward Calculation

Symbol	Entry	Type	Shares	Stop	Target
GG	$35.33	Long	100	$30.00	$46.00

R/R Ratio	Loss Risk	Profit Potential	Pattern
1 to 2.5	-$533.00	$1,067.00	Up Trend

Looking at these calculations, it's obvious that the FXE is the better trade, right? It carries a reward of 2.5 while GG is only 2. To understand if FXE really is the better trade, determine the *real rate of return*. Think about it this way, you want to take a trade only if the following occur:

- The risk-to-reward makes sense (1:2 minimum; 1:3 or more preferably).

- You can give the trade enough room to move around without stopping out (normal trading range over the period of time you are invested in the stock).

- The trade taken offers the best real rate of return (assuming all other things are equal like the risk of the trade failing for example) with the least risk to your capital.

So far in the calculations, the real rate of return has not been a consideration. Instead, only the risk-to-reward was considered. To understand this difference, the risk-to-reward matrix needs another component – time.

Here's the same risk-to-reward tables with an added column – *Expected Duration*, which is meant to imply the expected time it should take for the two trades to complete.

Table 10 - Risk-to-Reward with Time as a Calculation Component

Symbol	Entry	Type	Shares	Stop	Target	Pattern
FXE	$157.92	Short	100	$160.21	$152.21	Resistance

R/R Ratio	Loss Risk	Profit Potential	Expected Duration
1 to 2.5	-$229.00	$571.00	10 days

Symbol	Entry	Type	Shares	Stop	Target	Pattern
GG	$35.33	Long	100	$30.00	$46.00	Up Trend

R/R Ratio	Loss Risk	Profit Potential	Expected Duration
1 to 2	-$533.00	$1,067.00	60 days

Using the added knowledge of how long the trade is expected to take, another calculation can occur that indicates the real rate of return on the trade (as shown below in Table 11).

Table 11 - Risk-to-Reward showing Real Rate of Return

Symbol	Entry	Type	Shares	Stop	Target	Pattern
FXE	$157.92	Short	100	$160.21	$152.21	Resistance

R/R Ratio	Loss Risk	Profit Potential	Expected Duration	Rate of Return
1 to 2.5	-$229.00	$571.00	10 days	.362%

Symbol	Entry	Type	Shares	Stop	Target	Pattern
GG	$35.33	Long	100	$30.00	$46.00	Up Trend

R/R Ratio	Loss Risk	Profit Potential	Expected Duration	Rate of Return
1 to 2	-$533.00	$1,067.00	60 days	.503%

The calculation of the real rate of return is computed from the expected profit potential and is shown below:

Return on Equity = Profit Potential / (Entry Price * Number of Shares)

Real Rate of Return = Return on Equity / Expected Duration

Applying these calculations, the Real Rate of Return for FXE is

Return on Equity = $571 / ($157.92 * 100) = 3.62%

Real Rate of Return = 3.62 / 10 days
$$= .362\% \text{ per day}$$

Doing the same calculations for GG, the results are a bit surprising:

Return on Equity = $1067 / ($35.33 * 100) = 30.20%

Real Rate of Return = 30.20% / 60 days

$$= .503\% \text{ per day}$$

Now that the calculations are complete, it becomes clearer that FXE is not really the best trade to be had since GG returns a higher real rate of return. This is true even though FXE is a much shorter trade in duration.

Many times the real rate of return calculation ends up pretty surprising. There are times when the unlikely trade becomes the better deal due to the concept of time. For example, if the FXE trade was expected to take only 5 days to complete, the calculation results in a real rate of return of .724% per day. Suddenly, the FXE looks to be the better trade.

Return on Equity = $571 / ($157.92 * 100) = 3.62%

Real Rate of Return = 3.62 / 5 days

$$= .724\% \text{ per day}$$

This is true because the faster you turn your money around and put it into the next trade, the greater the returns.

Note: The key determinate in the value of the real rate of return lies in a reasonably

Unfortunately, estimating trade time durations is not a science. It comes with experience and practice. Additionally, as discussed later (see *Trade Data - your Trading Diary*), analyzing your past data enables you to predict the future length of trades with greater accuracy and it is there that you can actually become a better estimator of the best potential trade.

How Much Capital to Commit to the Trade

Another important decision you have to make is how large the trade should be. Do you buy 100 shares of GG and sell short 100 shares of FXE? How about 200 shares of GG and 400 shares of FXE? Clearly you are limited to how much capital you have in your trading account, but what other factors play into the decision making process of how large you should trade?

There are many different strategies governing the size of a trade and the resultant risk exposure to your overall portfolio. A simple rule of thumb is that you seldom allow one position to create risk greater than about 2%

---

[51] Choosing the best available trade (though highly dependent on trade duration estimation), also depends on all the other assumptions such as your stop loss and target placement. All are factors in the calculation.

of your overall portfolio value. This is a back-of-the-envelope, seat-of-the-pants type approach.

There are formal approaches as well. How rigid and formal you are depends a lot on how rigid you are as a trader. Regardless of whether you are quite formal in your approach or not, understanding the thinking that goes behind the formal approach is useful. So here are some guidelines:

$$s = \frac{e \cdot r}{p \cdot x}$$

Where:

   s = size of the trade

   e = portfolio equity (cash and holdings)

   r = maximum risk percentage per trade

   p = entry price on the trade

   x = pre-determined stop loss or exit price

The best way to understand this formula is through a simple example. Let's use the stock GG that is being considered for the trade. From the previous discussions, GG has support at $30 so that's where the stop loss order will be. Assuming your overall portfolio size is $30,000; multiply that by the amount of risk you are willing to take on this one trade. Let's assume that to be 2%. The result of this calculation is $600.

Now take the entry price of GG and the pre-determined stop loss area of $30 which yields $5.33 per share of risk. Finally, divide the $600 from above by $5.33 (risk) to equal 112.5, or roughly 113 shares that can be bought using these parameters.

Naturally you are not going to do this rigid math for each trade you make. In reality, you do the math once, and then estimate after that until your portfolio grows or shrinks by some significant amount. Once you know you can risk about $600 per trade, you see how much you are risking per share and quickly estimate the number of shares you can/should trade.

Typically, traders think that the way they increase their returns is to increase the size of their trades. This again is not only incorrect, but it is also deadly. Increasing the size of your trades usually increases your risk at a proportional rate. The preferable way to increase your gains is either decreasing the time you are in a trade or trading more volatile instruments (with a smaller amount of capital). Let me quickly explain.

Making trades where the outcome happens more quickly (on average) effectively increases your capital base through the magic of compounding (in this case, compounding returns over a shorter period of time). Consider these two examples:

In the first example, you purchase 100 shares of stock XYZ for $100 per share – or for $10,000 of your capital. In this example, let's say you keep the stock for one year and let's assume you make $10 per share for a total return of 10% for the year.

In the second example, you purchase 100 shares of XYZ for $100 per share and sell it for $105 per share. Do this 5 times for one year. Assuming that you have your capital tied up for the whole year in these five trades, your total return for the year is $25 per share for a total return of 25% for the year. In effect, you have increased your capital base by trading a bit more frequently.

Trading more volatile financial instruments with smaller size (like futures as a more extreme example) can increase your returns because you are able to trade the actual volatility itself.

> **Note: This is a more advanced topic and not one I will spend time on here. For now, stick with the idea of increasing the trade turnover and leave the more volatile trading for another day.**

Partial Buys and Sells

Large traders almost always make partial buys and sells. They do this for two reasons:

- They are buying or selling lots and lots of shares. In fact, unless the stock trades millions of shares on a daily basis, they have to buy and sell their shares in partial lots. Doing otherwise would abnormally affect the price causing large price spikes or dips that hurt them.

- Large traders know what most small traders do not recognize – that it is more profitable to buy and sell stocks on the way up and down rather than believing that you can somehow know where the high or low price will be. The reason for this is rather simple but not as well understood by the *little guy* – or at least not accepted by the small trader. Knowing the high or low price for a stock for some time frame implies that you are able to predict the future consistently; that's simply not going to happen.

Fortunately, stocks move up and down (not in a straight line), the vast majority of the time. Large traders use this fact to constantly pocket profits as stocks naturally move forward and back – from higher to lower prices and vice versa. The normal ebb and flow of the market provides the opportunity for traders to make additional profits regardless of whether they are large or small.

With low transaction costs and the ability to easily monitor positions and make trades, the little guy can mimic the large trader in today's market. The little guy can make their portfolio larger by actively managing the positions in it; taking profits and reducing losses by scaling in and out ... just like a big guy.

Making the Trade

All of the preliminary work is done and now it's time to make the trade. Given the analysis, the FXE sell order is ready for entry into the market. The desired size is 200 shares[52]. The plan is to do that in two purchases: scaling into half of the trade at the current price and the final half of the trade as FXE approaches the recent highs (if it in fact does so). If FXE doesn't trade higher, then the trade will end up being only 100 shares initially. Shares may be added later if the trade sets up further, but that is to be decided later.

So, a *good-till-cancelled limit order* to short sell 100 shares of FXE at $157.92 is entered while a second *good-till-cancelled limit order* to short sell 100 shares of FXE is entered at $159.81 – just over the previous high. The thought is that if the old high is breached, FXE should run higher as stop loss orders are triggered. By placing the second sell order at 30 basis points higher than the previous highs, I am banking on the round number of $160.00 to serve as resistance. Why

---

[52] With a $30,000 portfolio, I could have chosen to take a greater risk but given how close the stop is, the risk of a stop being hit makes you decide to keep the overall size of the risk smaller. If the trade works, it is going to be a very profitable trade as is.

$160.00? Because, for whatever reason, traders like round numbers and use them as stopping points when trading. It's psychological but consistently seen over and over again in the markets.

Finally, a *good-till-cancelled stop loss buy order* is placed at $160.21 as planned.

Note:	Each time you place an order to enter into a position, the corresponding buy or sell stop is also placed into the market – always! In this trade, the buy stop market order is placed for a total of 200 shares at a price point of $160.21, which corresponds to your risk-to-reward calculations.
	By short selling at two different times, the risk-to-reward parameters change more to your favor. If both orders execute, the resultant reward-to-risk parameters change to a $4.2 reward for each $1 of risk as shown in Table 12 below.

Table 12 - Revised FXE Short Trade - Risk-to-Reward Calculation

Symbol	Entry	Type	Shares	Stop	Target	Pattern
FXE	$158.66	Short	200	$160.21	$152.21	Resistance

R/R Ratio	Loss Risk	Profit Potential	Expected Duration
1 to 4.2	-$310.00	$1,290.00	10 days

Waiting for your Entry Point

The GG trade, however, is not quite ready and requires you to wait. A *good-till-cancelled limit order* to buy 100 shares of GG is placed at the round number $35, and a corresponding *good-till-cancelled stop loss sell order* for 100 shares is placed at $30.00 to protect you if your entry order is triggered. If the market trades to the price point where you want to make the purchase, then that is great. If it doesn't, there are several other gold stock trades to pursue. Never concern yourself with having to get into this or that trade – **there is always another trade.**

One of the more difficult tasks a trader faces is the temptation to chase a trade. You know the scenario. You've looked at the charts. The patterns are right. You are just itching to make this trade if the stock pulls back to the target purchase price, but rather than pulling back, the stock moves higher. You gasp! A big gulp and ... you pull the trigger, buying the stock 6 or 7% higher than where you wanted to enter the trade. What are you doing?

You are setting yourself up for failure! Why would you do such a thing? Well, as all traders know, when in the thick of battle, your emotions become the enemy. The tendency to make a trade on an emotional basis is tremendous. That is why it is so important to do your homework when the market isn't open; to calculate your potential entry and exit points and to enter those points into your spreadsheet and choose the few trades you expect to concentrate upon next. Buying a stock 50 basis points higher than you previously calculated could make the difference between a profitable trade and an unprofitable one. It certainly changes your risk-to-reward equation and it is an indication that you are not patient enough. Patience on entry is a key concept!

So, how can you allow a trade to pass you by? What is the emotional crutch needed to become a patient trader?

The primary one that you can use is to tell yourself that there are many fish in the pond and that it isn't necessary to catch every fish that swims by in order to be successful. In fact, it's only necessary to catch those few that bite. If you are using the standard tools that each trader should have in their toolbox to search out trading opportunities (revisit the *Trade Idea Generation* section for a refresher for the tools available if needed), the opportunities will almost always be plentiful. The difficulty in trading typically is not in finding trading opportunities, but instead in choosing among them. There are always trades to be made. Don't concern yourself with that. Concern yourself with getting good entry points. If a stock doesn't want to bite, then don't worry about it. Be patient. If the trade is going to happen, the stock will provide the setup that allows you to enter into the trade – if not now, then later. If it

188

doesn't, pursue the other trades that are available. The risk-to-reward doesn't favor the missed trade as much as the other trades that do meet your criteria. **Always put the odds in your favor!**

You're In the Trade

Figure 24 is the chart of the FXE two days after placing your short sell order. The trade opened higher and the initial short sell executed immediately. In fact, in the two day period, both short sell orders executed.

Figure 24 - FXE Two Days Later

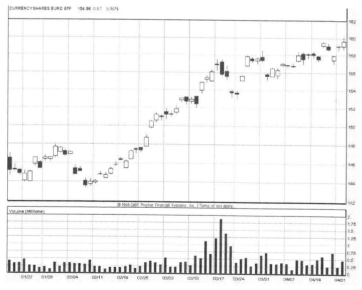

As the Euro heads higher, GG begins to fall again. Although GG is heading lower, it has yet to trigger your buy order.

Figure 25 - GG Two Days Later

Management of the Trades

Patient trading is a tough act to master. Patience is a personal characteristic most people find difficult to achieve, especially traders. In stock trading, people typically think of patience (as it applies to trading) as being associated with what you do after purchasing a stock – you hold onto it as long as is necessary to make a profit, then you sell it. If that's how you think of patience, reconsider it.

Patience is all about the following:

- Waiting on a stock to do what you expect it to do and provide you with the setup you want.
- Monitoring the trades you are in and those that you want to enter into, and constantly considering what might go wrong.
- Listening to what the market says and what it does. Doing so adds to your confidence and to the trades at hand as well as to the larger thesis/bias that you are trading with.
- Giving the stock time to do what it should do to fulfill your trading plan, yet not being lulled to sleep if it goes on longer than you expect. A patient trader is a trader who waits for a stock to start moving again in the expected direction after it turns stagnant. It also is about trimming your positions if the uncertainty or risk becomes too great.

The ability to exhibit patience is directly related to the amount of risk exposure you carry – the more risk you carry, the less patient you become. Although it is extremely important to show patience in entering and managing a trade, it is equally important to exhibit discipline with respect to risk as well. That is why you put your stop in **when you put a trade on**. It is why you **never move the stop** such that you increase your risk unless that was initially part of the trading plan. If your protection order is in the market and if you don't change it, you won't turn patience into stubbornness. It is why you sometimes trim positions prior to the position reaching your desired or target profit price objectives.

If events dictate a change in posture, a patient trader will listen to what the market is saying and will modify their stance to accommodate the new information that the market has released. You always must listen to the market and observe how it is acting. When it validates your thesis – great! Your conviction regarding your trade increases. When it begins to invalidate your thesis, then your conviction begins to wane. In that case, you must move to reduce exposure or exit prematurely if need be. There's nothing that says you have to wait until a stop loss order is executed if the market begins to tell you that what you expected to happen is no longer the most likely outcome.

One week later, GG triggers your *good-till-cancelled limit buy order* for 100 shares.

Figure 26 - GG One Week Later

During this same week, the FXE position has moved nicely in the direction desired. You breathe a sigh of relief as your *stop loss limit buy order* was not executed and your hedge trade is in place and at the price points you envisioned.

Figure 27 - FXE One Week Later

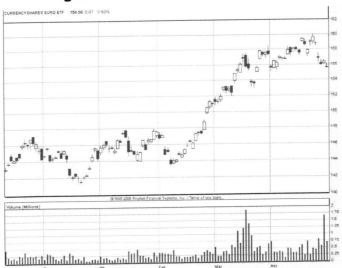

At this point, if you are practicing active money management, you are already taking the steps necessary to turn your good fortune into better fortune. Remember, active money management *means* actively managing the positions you have.

Taking Partial Profits

Since the FXE position has moved as desired, and now that you have also entered the GG position, you should be monitoring the progression of your positions on a daily basis. Once a position is entered, observe the position and calculate where the next resistance and

194

support levels lie. Depending on what technical method you use, how you make this calculation may differ from trader to trader. Regardless of the methods used, recalculate these resistance points daily as the chart continues to develop. Each day the market reveals more about the future course of the trade. The market is always releasing information about each and every stock that comprises the market.

Although you may think this amount of work isn't necessary because you are now simply waiting to get the full price extension before taking profits (as argued several times already) greater profits are realized by using the ebb and flow of the market to take and book partial profits along the way. There are those who will say that taking profits leads to poor results, but what they should have said was that "taking partial profits *prematurely* leads to poor results." Well, maybe, but not in my trading philosophy. Booking gains on your way to the ultimate price target and attempting to reestablish those same positions at more favorable price points is a validated methodology. When it comes to keeping your portfolio at or near its record levels, this is the way to do it and that is our overall trading strategy.

Ever since the FXE trade chart hit the $160 level, it has backed straight down for five straight days and almost 3% decline without so much as one bounce.

Now there's nothing that says it cannot go further, but consider the trade you have placed – long a gold stock

(GG) and short the Euro. In the present market conditions, the normal situation is that if the Euro moves lower in price, gold will follow. If gold depreciates, gold stocks will have greater difficulty in moving higher. In fact, the reason that GG hit your buy target is because the Euro was falling like a rock during this short time frame.

When trying to decide where you might take partial profits, I have found that it is best if you treat the decision just as you would an initial trade. Stop and ask yourself, "Given today's chart, at what price would you short sell the FXE and at what price point would you place your buy stop and target exit price?"

Although this is a continuation trade, treating it as a new trade forces you to be realistic about where support and resistance are without the mental overhang of the existing position (regardless of whether it is a good or bad trade). Looking at the chart again (see Figure 27) given the price drop, your risk now looks to be around $158.52 and the reward continues to be the $152.21 target originally set. To make this trade work on a 1:2 risk to reward ratio, the entry price for a subsequent short sell trade needs to be around $156.42 as shown below.

Table 13 - FXE Short Trade – Partial Profits Risk-to-Reward Calculation

Symbol	Entry	Type	Shares	Stop	Target	Pattern
FXE	$156.42	Short	100	$158.52	$152.21	Resistance

R/R Ratio	Loss Risk	Profit Potential	Expected Duration
1 to 2	-$210.00	$421.00	10 days

With the current price at $155.52, closing the trade here just doesn't make sense. You need to close it somewhere between $154.00 and $154.42. At that price point a sufficient incentive exists to risk that FXE simply continues lower and never provides you the ability to reestablish the additional 100 shares that you buy back when taking partial profits. Remember, when the trade is working in your favor and you want to take partial profits, you have to consider where you would re-enter the trade. That is the primary determinant as of where to take partial profits. If you cannot gain enough of a spread between where you would close the trade and subsequently re-enter the same trading position, then there is no reason to take profits yet. The risk of exiting and not realistically being able to get back in at a better price point should keep you in the trade unless there are other mitigating factors.

Given your homework, however, you know you have some reasonable parameters in hand to guide you on where it makes sense to take partial profits. The next day you enter a *limit buy day order* on the FXE for half the shares after the market opens. Since the Euro chart shows us that the Euro tends to gap up or gap down with regularity, you should wait until the market reopens to see where the stock opens before placing the order[53]. The order is placed just above the low at $154.50. You do this each day as long as the chart continues to show this as a favorable trade.

Two days later, the partial profit taking order on the FXE triggers and you book your profits. You move the existing *good-till-cancelled stop market order* of 200 shares lower in price to reflect your newly computed stop loss price point of $158.52 (see Table 13).

You don't need to reduce the size of your *stop loss order* because you immediately enter your new *good-till-cancelled limit short sell order* for FXE at $156.42 to reestablish the 100 shares you just bought back. Additionally, at this juncture, you enter an *order to take profits at* $152.21 for the 100 remaining shares you have remaining on the books. Since that price point is

---

[53] Notice that these are the things you learn by watching how a stock trades over time. Since the FXE trades off of the FOREX Euro, it trades almost 24 hours a day. How it trades in Europe greatly affects how it starts trading in New York once the New York market opens for trades. That is why the chart shows many gap up and gap down patterns.

close enough, being proactive and placing the *good-till-cancelled limit buy order* into the market is prudent. If FXE gaps lower to that price area, you want to take the remaining profits because the likelihood of the price continuing even lower without some sort of a retrace higher becomes even greater.

Now consider what you have done and the logic behind taking partial profits comes into full view. As a result of taking partial profits, you have dramatically changed the risk-to-reward dynamics of your FXE trade. In this particular case, you have put $416 dollars (less minor commissions) into your pocket and you have reduced your risk on the remaining shares to zero. You have guaranteed yourself an overall profit on this entire trade even if you were to re-enter the trade at $156.42 and were stopped out of all the shares you held.

The best is yet to come though. If FXE continues to trade lower without a bounce, and you do not re-enter, you would still end up with good profits. They will not be as great as they would have been had you not taken partial profits – but still good. If FXE does bounce, however, and if that bounce carries far enough for you to re-enter, you have the potential for even greater gains than originally planned. Essentially, you have created a win-win situation for yourself and you have done this without risking any additional capital. You have increased your profit potential with less risk overall.

If you do not take a trade unless your reward is at least twice as large as your risk and you combine that with partial profit taking, then you have put yourself in a very strong position to make money over time. You would have to be very unlucky or a terrible stock picker to lose in such a situation.

This is the essence behind active money management – always seeking reduced risks while increasing the profit potential on trades that are working with the win-win partial profit taking strategy. Following this formula, you will be able to keep your portfolio at or near its highs.

Adjusting Stops and Target Prices

Before continuing on with this trade, I want to emphasize the concept of constantly monitoring your positions. In the two trades you currently are engaged in, the FXE trade moved to your advantage and offered the opportunity to take some partial profits. In doing so, you reduced your risk and created a win-win scenario that you are always seeking as a trader. This active monitoring and money management strategy not only occurs for winning trades, but also for those trades that do not realize their potential.

There will always be trades where you do your homework and make the trade, but the stock becomes stagnant. It does not move significantly in either direction. As a result, you neither stop out of the position with a loss, nor do you reach a price point where partial profits can be realized (as was done with the FXE trade). Regardless, as the chart develops, constantly monitor the chart for any clues as to what is most likely to occur next. You do this by mentally divorcing yourself as a stock owner and instead asking yourself, "Given the current view that the charts provide, would I make this trade today?"

If the answer is no, consider how to reduce your risk in the trade since your confidence has decreased. To reduce your risk, you specifically look for the most favorable price point where you can remove some of your shares. That price point may be either at a slight profit, at breakeven, or even at a small loss, but if you do not have confidence in the trade, why allow it to potentially get worse? There's nothing that says that you have to stay in a trade to the bitter end. Remember, your *stop loss order* is there for protection. You do not put a *stop loss order* in with the hope that it will be hit. You place the order into the market to protect yourself and you constantly monitor the position with the idea of decreasing risk! If, over time, the trade no longer appears worthwhile, take some of your position off – reduce your risk and free up your capital.

On a related note, you should constantly be looking to adjust your stops and targets as the market evolves over time. Again, as the chart fills out, support and resistance points that may not have previously existed or were not obvious when you entered the trade are now revealed to you. If you decide that this is a trade you have little confidence in, use the added knowledge the chart provides to reduce your risk or to take partial profits without the idea of re-entering the trade. Always consider how to reduce risk at every turn, but do it in a manner that is consistent with a patient trading style. If there's nothing wrong with the trade and the chart doesn't reveal any reason to change your outlook, then leave the trade alone and give it time to develop.

Finally, there are three things that move a market – time, price and volume. Most people can grasp that price and volume (although many are confused by just how volume works) move markets, but few have an appreciation for how time affects the markets. Using the FXE trade as an example, note that it has moved lower in price by some 3% in five days, which given the historical volatility of this ETF, is a reasonably significant amount. When a stock moves too far *too fast,* it typically takes a rest. That rest may play out in one of three ways. In the case currently described:

1. The stock might continue lower in price, but at a slower pace.
2. Another possibility is that the stock may just move more-or-less sideways in price for a few days while it rejuvenates itself and prepares for a continuation move.

3. A final possibility is that the stock reverses in direction to work off some of the excess that it has developed. This latter case is typically what happens.

Time has a way of removing the excess that occurs in price moves. Time is the great arbiter in the market. In a manner of speaking, time makes the excess reasonable. The excess that occurs in the markets are almost always the result of emotions becoming extreme. Time allows those emotions to find a greater balance allowing the rational side of traders to reappear.

If you want to be successful in trading, commit the time and energy needed to develop a regimen where you monitor your positions on a daily basis. Consider whether to adjust your *stop loss orders* and/or your target profit *limit sell/buy orders*. While making those decisions, consider where partial profits should be taken, when losses should be taken, where re-entry orders should be placed, etc.

Giving the Position Time to Develop

In the two trades you have entered, FXE was timed almost perfectly. Fortunately for you, the timing on the GG trade appears almost as good. Two weeks into the trade, the charts now appear as shown below. Remember, for the GG trade, the original calculation called for a stop at $30 and a target of $46. The stock is now trading at $39.47. Doing a quick calculation, that means GG has risen some 18% off the bottom. That's quite a move in the span of five days[54]. Again, each day you should perform calculation of where partial profits can be taken. Also determine where potential re-entry trades can be made. This is not time for laziness but instead vigilance.

Figure 28 - GG - Two Weeks Later

---

[54] In previous examples, when FXE moved 3% in 5 days; that was a lot. Here you have GG moving 18% in five days and it points out an important concept – how far a stock can advance or retrace in some period of time is relative to the stock. You should not compare a percentage move in one stock with that of other stocks. Instead compare it to itself historically.

Looking at the GG chart (see Figure 28), support now looks to be that higher volume bar on May 8th (second bar from the right) and again at $36 where several lows were made over the past six weeks. If you were to enter this trade now, a purchase just above that $38 level with a stop just under the $36 support area would provide a nice purchase point for a new trade. Note that I am suggesting that your *stop loss sell order* no longer needs to be so low *because the chart has changed* since you first entered the trade. Take the information that the market has released to you and use it to reduce your risk. Thus, as a result of your observations, move your *stop loss sell order* up from the current $30 level to the $35.81 level – leaving some wiggle room for prices just below where support now exists.

Since the target price of $46 remains valid, use the new values the market has provided to decide if you might be able to capture partial profits in GG and attempt to reestablish yourself at a better price point in the near future. With GG now trading at almost $40, what if you sold half your shares at this price point and then attempted to repurchase them just above the support at $38? Would that provide another win-win situation (see Table 14)?

Table 14 - GG Re-Entry Risk-to-Reward Calculation

Symbol	Entry	Type	Shares	Stop	Target	Pattern
GG	$38.09	Long	50	$35.81	$46.00	Up Trend

R/R Ratio	Loss Risk	Profit Potential	Expected Duration
1 to 3.47	-$114.00	$395.50	10 days

To exit GG here and to use the newly calculated stop loss criterion yields a re-entry price point that has a reasonably good chance of getting triggered. The gain to be had, if all works according to plan, is to sell GG at $39.91 and attempt to repurchase it at $38.09 yielding a little less than $2 a share gain, or $100 on 50 shares. The change to your overall risk-to-reward would be significant though.

Regardless of whether you sell a partial position, you have already moved your stop loss order up to $35.81 because the market has released more information to you since you entered the trade. The situation has changed. The market dynamics for this trade are no longer what they were when you entered the trade. Given these changing dynamics, it makes sense to try and capture partial profits here, so you enter a *good-till-cancelled limit sell order* for 50 shares of GG on the following day at $39.91.

If the partial profit order is triggered at $39.91, immediately place your repurchase order (buy 50 shares of GG at the $38.09 *limit price, good-till-cancelled*). Leave your *good-till-cancelled stop loss order* for 100 shares at $35.81 because your repurchase order will necessarily trigger before your stop loss order.

You have now created the conditions for a win-win trade on GG. At this point, the worst case is that you stop out at $35.81 on the entire 100 shares. The good news is that even if that happens, you will have made money. You cannot lose unless the stock gaps down and overnight risk is realized (refer to the section on *Overnight Risk* as a refresher). The plan remains the same; reduce risk, exploit gains, and try to increase those gains further when they are working to your advantage.

The FXE trade (see Figure 29), on the other hand, has not retraced sufficiently to allow re-entry. Again, patience is required. A successful trader **must** exhibit patience when trading. So much of trading is waiting. If you have done your homework, you know the price points for the trades you want to make. You cannot allow emotions to override your discipline. Emotions are your enemy when trading. Stay cool, calm, and collected. Having prepared beforehand, you know what you are looking for and you have to maintain discipline and wait for that scenario to develop. Until the market releases additional information that changes your viewpoint about where support and resistance lie, wait.

This continuing release of information is something you have to constantly factor into your decision making regarding your target price and stops. It is a bad trade to prematurely take profits or losses due to a lack of patience, but it is equally wrong to ignore any new information the market has released.

If your idea of portfolio management is to do the homework for trade establishment then sit back and wait, you are being gravely naïve about what is required to be successful. Active portfolio management entails a constant evaluation of where you have been, where you currently are, and where you are likely going with respect to the positions you hold. It is active!

Figure 29 - FXE - Two Weeks Later

FXE and GG – The Trade Continues

Another week passes and you were fortunate to capture the partial sale of GG and take those profits to the bank. That trade triggered Monday, May 12th at $39.91, yielding a profit of $4.58 per share or $229.00 total (less commissions). Per your plan, you immediately placed a re-entry order (*good-till-cancelled limit buy order*) at $38.09 for the 50 shares you just sold. Given the volatility, your re-entry order actually triggered the very next day. At this point, you have the full 100 share lot of GG once more. Just like with the FXE trade, you now have the win-win trade situation you were seeking.

Your average cost for the 100 shares you are holding amounts to $36.71[55]. If your *stop loss order* is triggered at $35.81, you stand to lose $0.90 on the remaining shares or a total of $90.00 plus commissions. Remember that you have already pocketed $229.00 on the partial sale so; once again, you cannot lose on the trade. Here's the GG chart updated three weeks since entering the initial trade.

Figure 30 - GG - Three Weeks Later

---

[55] The remaining 50 shares purchased at $35.81 + the 50 newly added shares at $38.09.

Once again, during this week of trading, the market has released additional information to you. The strength in the GG chart (where prices quickly appreciated even higher once you re-entered the trade) is apparent. From lows to highs, GG has gained $8 in 10 trading days or 23% (which is quite significant). The chart informs us that, on a short-term basis, support at $38 is real (the stock was quickly bought again when prices retreated to that level; volume tapered off as prices retreated from $40 to $38. It expanded again as prices surged over the highs just above $40). This informs you that $40 is now the higher support area, but given the sudden rise in prices, the stock could still retreat to $38 and have nothing wrong with it. Use this new information to your advantage.

Let's consider how you use this new information (that the market has released) to manage the increasing risk of a stock that is moving higher at a rapid pace. For example, at this juncture you could take one of several differing actions – each of which carries a different amount of risk and reward. Your options include:

- Place an order to sell the entire position at the original target price of $46.00 and wait.

- Continue to try taking partial profits as the stock moves higher (to an identified resistance area) and then try to reestablish those positions as the stock moves back lower (to an identified support area).

- Take partial profits on the way up and do *not* re-establish positions on a pull back because the risks are too great.
- Take all the profits now and look for another trade.

The above are always your options on a stock that continues to perform. As a stock moves too-far-too-fast, the odds of it continuing its move become less and less likely to occur. It doesn't mean that it can't continue – just that it has a lower probability of doing so. How far is too-far-too-fast? It depends on the stock. Some move faster than others as seen with GG and FXE. As discussed previously, you surmise this by looking at a chart or checking the stock's beta. For GG, we see from its recent history that it can easily move $10 in a straight line fashion – it did it in March (from $46 to just over $36 in four days) and again in April (from $43.41 to $33.81 in twelve days). On this current move, GG has moved from $33.81 to $41.97 in twelve days. Considering both time and price, you have to assume that this rapid price appreciation is more likely nearing an end rather than a beginning. Common sense tells you that.

Using this information, it seems you should consider taking some additional profits. There really isn't a reason to remove the trade because *there's nothing in the charts to suggest anything is wrong with GG.* In fact, everything suggests that GG is doing quite well. Remember, be patient. Let the trade work for you. It's good portfolio management to reduce risks and to book gains, but don't cut your gains off. Let the stock tell you when it's done.

The chart indicates that the swing high of $43.41 is the likely target for this current move (again refer to Figure 30). This assumption is based on:

- The length of the previous move (twelve days).
- The distance the stock has traveled ($8.16 so far).
- The fact that $43.41 is only $1.44 away from today's high.

An additional consideration is a what-if scenario. What if GG doesn't take a rest and just continues on to the old highs. How likely would it be at that point that it continues even higher? Less likely is the correct answer. Given that, what are the odds that you could reestablish the trade on a retrace (pull back) to the $43.41 area if that happens? The answer is, of course, reasonably likely. Given this rationalization, the odds are that you would most likely be able to re-establish a position (if you so choose) at or near where you exit, even if you are wrong about the ultimate strength of this stock in the current short term time frame.

Using the above logic put a *good-till-cancelled limit buy order* to sell 50 shares at $43.31. Considering the current chart, support is reasonably solid at $38 so, consequently, you move your stop for 100 shares to

$37.81, leaving some room for error. The risk-to-reward ratio of 1:2 requires a retrace to $40.54 to re-establish the position, if partial profits are taken (as shown in Table 15).

Table 15 – GG Re-Entry Risk-to-Reward Calculation (second re-entry)

Symbol	Entry	Type	Shares	Stop	Target	Pattern
GG	$40.54	Long	50	$37.81	$46.00	Up Trend

R/R Ratio	Loss Risk	Profit Potential	Expected Duration
1 to 2	-$136.50	$273.00	10 days

With the FXE trade, little has happened. The price is moving higher, but it has yet to trigger your re-entry price point. There is nothing on the chart (refer to Figure 31) that alarms you, so you simply wait.

Figure 31 - FXE - Three Weeks Later

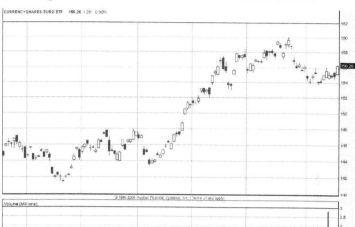

At the end of four weeks, the FXE trade actually triggers your short sell order (remember you had placed it at $156.42) and is threatening both your existing and newly established short positions at the *good-till-cancelled buy stop order* of $158.52. Now you have to have nerves of steel and count on your research to serve you well. Looking at the chart (see Figure 32), you can see how close you are now to the stop loss order as the prices just shot higher and have reached as high as $158.34. This is where you are tempted to remove the stop loss order or at least to move it up higher so it won't be triggered. You have all weekend to think about it, and that makes it much more difficult. Your stop loss could be triggered first thing Monday morning

215

if the Euro trades higher in Europe prior to the NYSE opening on Monday. This is where a trader has to make the *right* decision.

Figure 32 - FXE - Four Weeks Later

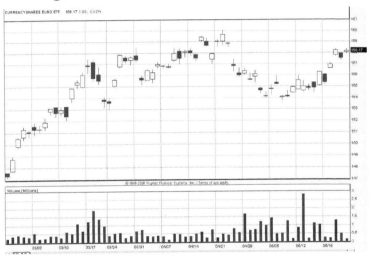

The problem is that every trader, when faced with a position that is not going according to plan, unless they are extremely disciplined, begins to re-examine their exit criteria. The thought process is something along the lines of, "Well, there is additionally support right above/below", or, "I can always buy/sell more and average down," or, "Surely this stock has extended too far, so it can't move against me much more. I don't want to kill it prematurely."

Notice how easy it is to rationalize the act of staying in a position that is moving against you and beyond your original exit criteria? It is agonizing to have a trade stop out, but it is a necessary part of disciplined trading. If you want to trade, you have to become unemotional with respect to the trades you make. Some work, and some don't. If you follow your discipline, half of all your trades could fail but you would still make money. This is accomplished because you only take the trades where your reward outweighs your risk on a 2-to-1 ratio (or greater). Even if you select lousy stocks, as long as you project a reasonably accurate picture of how much potential profit there is for the amount of risk you are willing to take, you are going to make money over time.

The moral of the story is that when you determine your entry and exit points, be honest with yourself. Sure, it's acceptable (actually it is advisable) to leave some wiggle room, but do your best to add that wiggle room into the original risk-to-reward equation. In other words, error on the side of being conservative on your exit for a winning trade, and error on the side of being generous on the exit of a losing trade. If you abide by these rules and if they are part of your original projections, you will succeed on average, over time. Unless and until the market releases information that may or may not result in modifications to those original projections, then stick with them. As a result, you leave the *stop loss order* alone.

GG, on the other hand, has rewarded you once more. The swing high partial profit target was triggered and prices reversed that same day. You again book partial profits. Since the eventual target price of $46.00 is reasonably close, placing a *good-till-cancelled sell order* for the remaining shares at that price point is prudent.

Figure 33 - GG - Four Weeks Later

Once again, consider whether it makes sense to again repurchase the shares you just sold. The calculations done in Table 15 indicated that $40.54 was the highest price point where a repurchase still yielded a 1:2 risk-to-reward ratio (assuming the $37.81 stop loss price and a $46 target price). Looking at the chart, those assumptions still remain valid so place the re-purchase *good-till cancelled buy order* for 50 shares in the market at $40.54, leaving your *stop loss order* the same.

At this point, your profits on GG amount to $564.00[56] and you still have 50 shares that are showing a $355.00 profit. Remember; when you started this trade you were risking $533.00 and shooting for a reward of $1067.00 (refer to Table 16). You are well on your way to achieving the original goal – and then some.

Table 16 – GG Risk-to-Reward Calculation (reprinted)

Symbol	Entry	Type	Shares	Stop	Target	Pattern
GG	$35.33	Long	100	$30.00	$46.00	Up Trend

R/R Ratio	Loss Risk	Profit Potential	Expected Duration	Rate of Return
1 to 2	-$533.00	$1,067.00	60 days	.503%

Surprisingly, the other trade (FXE) does not stop you out. Just when it appeared the stop would be triggered, prices reversed and dropped just as fast as they had risen (see Figure 34).

---

[56] Your average price for the shares was $36.71, and you sold half of those shares (50) at $43.31 resulting in a gain of $6.70 per share or $335.00. Adding that to the original $229.00, you have a gain of $564.00 so far.

Figure 34 - FXE - Five Weeks Later

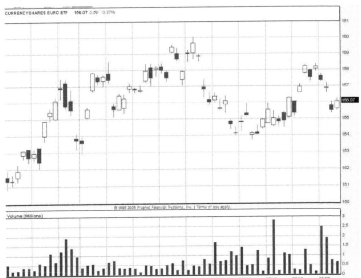

At this point, the market has released addition information to you. It is saying that your original resistance projections were indeed on target. It is also telling you that if and when FXE trades higher than $158.34, the prices will probably rise all the way back to the high of $160, if not further. Other than confirming your stop was well placed, the market has not moved sufficiently to demand that you do anything else, so it's back to waiting for now.

Looking back at the GG trade once more, that spike high that enabled you to sell was indeed a reversal. Subsequently, prices came back hard afterwards

220

triggering your re-entry order once more – this time at
$40.54. Has the market taught you anything more as a
result of trading this week (see Figure 35)?

Figure 35 - GG - Five Weeks Later

From a technical analysis perspective, what is
bothersome is that the FXE chart showed tremendous
volume as it broke lower and GG has shown higher
volume each time it came down (prior to May) as
opposed to going up. As a market technician, that is not

what you would prefer to see[57], and as a result, you might want to entertain the thought of trimming your GG positions here. With FXE so weak, that could restart the downtrend in GG.

Knowing When to Trim Your Positions

Although patience is required when monitoring an existing trade and waiting for it to develop, there is a downside to being too patient. Excessive patience can result in stubbornness, and that usually results in lost money and losing trades. Stubbornness is typically based on hope, and hope has no place in trading.

You can also be stubborn on a winning trade and end up giving back good gains. You should always consider – "What is the market telling me? Has the market released any useful information that I should use to reduce risk or to cut losses?"

In the GG example, the gap lower has you concerned. Uncertainty is always the trigger for you to consider trimming your position size. When the horizon can no longer be seen with any clarity, reduce your risk a bit

---

[57] There are many books that explain how to use volume numbers to confirm price movement. Refer again to Tom O'Brien and <u>Timing the Trade – Timing the Trade: How Price and Volume Move Markets</u>, Tiger Financial News Network, Inc., 1st Printing 2005.

and wait for the uncertainty to pass. Cash is a wonderful place to wait out a market because you can't lose when sitting on cash.

There doesn't have to be dire warnings or reasons to fear the trade – especially if you are in a winning position already. No, you don't want to cut your profits short and you shouldn't remove the entire trade, but you can remove some portion of it. By reducing your risk now while you have profits, you are actually increasing the odds that you can remain in the trade longer term. How? You can do this by reducing your position size and repositioning your stops back to a stronger support line previously used to reduce the possibility that they will trigger. If you wait, this will not make sense from a risk-to-reward perspective. If the trade turns worse, you have the added baggage of having to decide if you want to take losses on part of the trade rather than taking profits. Profits are always better in my book.

In the GG example, the last 50 share position was added at the $40.51 price point. A study of the chart indicates that the most you can likely sell these shares for is around $41 – if you exit now. Why not sell the recently added 50 shares, book some small gains, and re-evaluate next week after a few more days have traded? Uncertainty in this technical development would lead me to do so, and I recommend that you place a *good-till-cancelled limit sell order* for 50 shares of GG at $40.91. If the trade triggers, immediately change your *stop loss order* from 100 shares to 50 since you are uncertain if you intend to repurchase those 50 shares again.

Drawing the Trades to a Close

As the week progresses, GG does trigger your partial profit sell order at $40.91 enabling you once more to book some gains. Immediately afterwards, it threatens your stop loss order at $37.81 by trading as low as $38.15. Clearly the stock is developing a great volatility (up and down) in this higher price range (see Figure 36).

> **Note:** The hedge trades have now been in place for six weeks. The typical basing phase for a stock is six to nine weeks. Given that six weeks have passed, it is important to be keenly critical of price action at this phase of the trades and to keep risk minimized.

Figure 36 - GG - Six Weeks Later

On GG, you have half of the original trade still in place. There is no reason to increase that risk at this juncture. An examination of the latest chart patterns shows that volume flows are still OK and favorable but volatility continues to expand as GG works off its recent run to higher prices. You have to consider either removing the trade or giving the stop a little more leeway because that last drop in prices almost hit your stop order[58].

---

[58] Realize that a change in the stop price (lower) at this juncture is strictly in response to market conditions and comes after you have previously raised your stop loss order twice as the chart dictated that possibility

225

Since there is still nothing seriously wrong with the trading action in GG, moving the stop back to the previous placement at $35.81 (see Table 14) offers the best chance to stay in the GG trade for the possibility of a longer term increase in price. Eventually you know that either the FXE trade or the GG trade will fail – they are a hedge after all. Once the trading range that you have exploited fails, one side or the other of the trade will also fail. That is why you are reducing risk and attempting to error on the side of caution. The attempt is to stay in each of the trades as long as possible – preferably until they unequivocally inform you that the spread trade is no longer viable.

The FXE trade (see Figure 37) has once more moved back to threaten your *stop loss order*. Once more you have to leave the order in place, but this most recent threat informs you that the original profit target seems less and less unattainable.

previously. You would not consider moving your *stop loss order* lower if you had not previously raised it and taken partial profits.

Figure 37 - FXE - Six Weeks Later

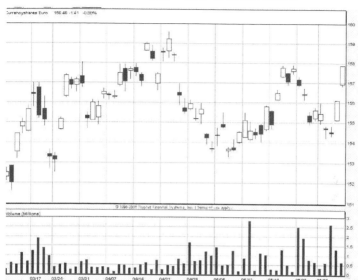

Revisiting the FXE chart, over the past six weeks, FXE has moved as low as $153.30 in early May and then only as low as $154.22 the in early June. The highs experienced during that same time frame were $157.88 (the third week of May) and now $157.63 (in early June). Since you want to reduce your risk at this juncture, you have to realize that taking partial profits in the low $154 area is probably the right thing to do if you don't get stopped out before that possibility. This way, you can reduce risk consistent with the six-to-nine week basing period and keep a reduced amount of stock in both FXE and GG on hand until one or the other breaks out of their respective trading range.

As a result, you place a *good-till-cancelled limit sell order* for 100 shares of FXE at $154.51. If the order triggers, you should change the existing stop order to 100 shares from 200 shares.

The following week, the partial profit triggers once more on the FXE trade (see Figure 38) placing another profit of $191.00[59]. You change the *stop loss order* for the remaining shares to 100 shares and once again move to the wait and watch mode.

Figure 38 - FXE – Seven Weeks Later

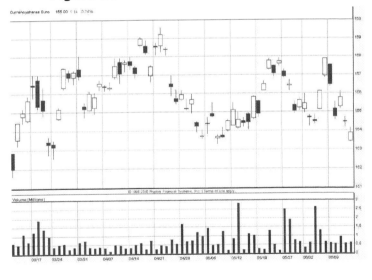

---

[59] A profit of $191.00 was realized based on the re-entry price of $156.42 for 100 shares ($156.42-$154.51) * 100 shares.

At this juncture, it is time to remove the profit target orders and to wait for one side of the trade to inform us which one is going to win. If you are fortunate, one side will show us its true intentions but the other won't stop out. If that happens, you should look to take profits on the side that appears to eventually lose. Next, either ride the winning position or potentially begin to add to that position on retraces and look to take profits on expansions much as you have done previously.

After ten weeks, GG flashes a green light – it wants to break higher (see Figure 39). It takes out the previous highs at $46.24 as volume surges. This is the signal you have been waiting for. Although it could be a false breakout, given the volume surge and confirmation of higher prices both in the GLD ETF and other gold stocks, it appears to be genuine.

Figure 39 - GG - Ten Weeks Later

The first action to take is to move your *stop loss order* higher because if the breakout to new highs is legitimate, the support area just below $40 should now hold onto any retrace near term. The next consideration is whether you intend to add more shares on any subsequent retrace. You perform your risk-to-reward calculations and make your decisions.

The other matter to deal with is the FXE trade because it still has not triggered your *stop loss order* at $158.52. Ideally you would like to remove the remnants of this trade at the best possible price point because you now believe that it is destined to fail in the next few days of trading given what GG has done. Looking at the current chart (see Figure 40), the best bet opportunity to exit near term is somewhere between $156.00 and $157.00 assuming you don't get stopped out first. Remove the two existing orders for FXE and enter a *one cancels the other order* to buy 100 shares of FXE at $158.52 or at $156.83. If the market (FXE) provides that last retrace before it spurts higher in price (which is common), you can exit with more money in your pocket on the short sell and with the promise of GG still trading higher.

Figure 40 - FXE - Ten Weeks Later

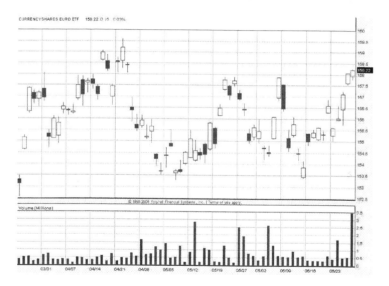

> **Note:** The trades used to exemplify *active money management* were not finalized by the time this book was completed and are left open ended with stops in place and an

> OCO order to remove the FXE short sell trade.
>
> Ideally, if GG proves to be a true breakout, a trader would then purchase additional shares on a pull back with an intermediate term target of approximately $56 to $57 (calculated by taking the highs plus the span of the range the shares have traded in recently).

When to Trade Larger and Smaller

As I discussed previously (see *How Much Capital to Commit to the Trade*), you should strive to keep the size of your trades roughly equal in terms of risk. If you have a $50K portfolio, you should not allow any trade to claim more than about $1000 – or about 2%.

Decreasing your trading size is a good practice when you are struggling. Many times you will find that after a few bad trades, you become very anticipatory about the next trade – to the point where you don't even give the trade a chance to succeed. As soon as you get a small profit or loss, you take it. This leads to overtrading and exceptionally bad results since you are breaking the rules you are attempting to use. Sometimes it is best to back down and reduce the size of your trades so that the risk of loss is smaller and therefore you can relax and let the trade have the needed time to work. It becomes a confidence builder. Trading smaller enables you to regain your confidence to the point where you can trade normal sized trades again. Trading is a game of confidence. If you lack confidence, your performance suffers. Back off and trade smaller until you regain your confidence.

Leverage and Margin

The concept of leverage and the practice of margin are interrelated. Leverage, in a pure sense, is the ability to control a group of assets whose value is greater than the amount of money you have actually used to secure those assets. True leverage, as it applies to a trader does not involve the added costs of interest payments – you are not borrowing in order to buy more than you otherwise could purchase with your existing capital. As a *little guy*, the only place you could do this historically was in the futures markets (commodities, FOREX, etc.).

Previously (see the section *Mixing Long and Short Positions in a Portfolio*), I discussed how the recent introduction of leveraged ETF products have quickly gained popularity. Current examples are the ProShares ETF securities. These offer a 2:1 leverage for indexes that track the prices of the general market indexes such as the S&P 500, the DJIA, the NASDAQ NDX, and the Russell 2000. These leveraged funds are typically offered in pairs: one that simulates the buying of shares in the underlying index, and one that simulates the selling of shares in the same underlying index. They have expanded the instruments that a non-margined account can purchase to include instruments that effectively short the underlying index by buying the cleverly constructed inverse ETF. So, not only have they allowed IRA accounts to effectively short the market, but they have allowed them to do it in a leveraged manner.

Margin, on the other hand, is the use of some third party's money (usually your broker) to buy and sell securities. To short sell securities, you have to have a margined account[60], but that's not the same thing as using margin money to buy something you otherwise would not have sufficient capital to accomplish. In the case of margin, your broker provides these additional funds and charges you interest to use the additional capital.

Why Would You Want to Leverage?

The primary reason for leveraging is rather obvious; to increase your profit potential without increasing your capital base. Consider a real-life example that you are probably engaged in at the moment. When you purchased your home, did you pay cash for the home or did you borrow? Most likely, you borrowed the vast majority of the purchase price.

---

[60] Short selling doesn't imply the use of margin. Instead it implies that you are borrowing money to buy or sell something that you otherwise would not have sufficient resources to do yourself.

If you think about it, what you have done is leveraged. You have used someone or some other institution's money to make a purchase that you otherwise could not have made. This leverage is likely to yield you a greater percentage gain once you sell the property. For example, assume that when you purchased your property, you paid $200,000 for it[61]. Furthermore, assume that you put 10% ($20,000) down when you made the purchase. In this example, you have a 10:1 leverage ratio – you control $200,000 worth of assets with only $20,000 down. If the property increases in value by $20,000, your gain is $20,000 on a $20,000 investment or 100%[62]. That's the power of leverage.

Of course leverage can work in reverse, which is what some homeowners in the current economy are finding out. If the home decreases 10% in value and you have leverage of 10:1, your loss becomes 100% of your investment capital. Ouch!

The exact same principle applies to these newer ETF vehicles although the leverage is 2:1. In the futures markets, however, a leverage ratio of 50:1 or more is commonplace. The ability to control a larger amount of

---

[61] For the sake of simplicity, assume your total costs include all closing costs, etc.

[62] For simplicity these figures ignore resale costs, interest charges, etc. They are intended to simply show what leverage is and the power of leverage.

assets than you would otherwise be able to do is what leverage is all about. Traders use leverage to increase their profit potential on a given trade beyond what they could otherwise do with their own money. The risk, of course, is that if you leverage to gain increased profit percentages, you carry the burden of increased loss percentages as well.

What are Risks and Rewards of Leveraging?

The risks and rewards of leveraging are directly related. The higher the increase in potential percentage rewards carries a corresponding higher potential for percentage loss. It's a two-edged sword. The only difference is that when you use margin money, your costs of capital increases because now you must pay interest on the money that you borrow. This increases your transactional costs and your desire to pick trades that are apt to move sooner rather than later (as time is money).

Why use Margin Money?

Margin money is useful to traders when short-term opportunities are available. Typically a broker does not charge for the use of margin money if the trade is both initiated and closed within the same trading day, although you generally need to have a sufficiently capitalized account to avoid SEC rules and penalties as explained previously (see *What is a Sufficiently Capitalized Account?*). If a trade sets up where the risks are reasonable and the expected duration of the trade is short, trading on margin money may prove prudent. The same is true of a trade where the risk-to-reward of the trade is highly favorable (a 5:1 or 10:1 reward to risk as an example) but you currently have all your capital already tied up in other trades. In such a case, you may decide to use margin money. These are valid cases.

When Not to Use Margin

In most situations, though, it is unwise to increase the cost of your trades by trading on margin. The use of margin money can become an addiction if you are not careful. You can start to depend on margin money to do everyday trades. If you are using margin money on a consistent basis, take a hard look at why you are doing so. Are you undercapitalized? Are you trying to hit home runs every time you make a trade? What are the situations that cause you to use margin money so often? In almost all cases, frequent use of margin money is likely to result in disaster. Avoid this practice.

Using Leverage

Beginning traders should avoid the use of leverage like the plague. It is certainly tempting to hit a home run on a 50:1 leveraged trade, but more often than not, the use of such leverage is most likely to result in a home run for the opposing team for which you'll be the one that ends up paying. The road to successful trading is scattered with failed home run hitters.

Once you have learned the ropes and truly understand sound money management principals as well as how to properly use leverage, consider its use. Until then – avoid it! Leverage is best when the risk factors are kept to a minimum, and that typically occurs by keep trading time frames very short. Until you are able to time your trades and consistently produce winners on very short time frames (no overnight exposure for example), then leverage should probably be left for another day.

Buying and Selling on Your Own Terms

Every investor and trader should strive to always place themselves in a position where they can buy and sell on their own terms. This is true for all types of investments, not just securities. To depend upon margin and leverage typically runs contrary to this principal. Successful traders always look to reduce risk by religiously protecting their capital. Leveraging your trades excessively does not make you a successful trader in the long run. Real money is made over time – not overnight. Sure there are the exceptions, but for those lucky few, there is a bounty of failed attempts.

Exiting the Trade

Stocks are like trees. To create the best forest it requires careful monitoring and an occasional pruning. All successful traders recognize that eventually you must exit the trade. Nothing lasts forever. So much is written about how to find the next great trade, but unfortunately few words have been written about how to exit them.

There are basically two ways to quit existing position:

- When the position reaches your target price and you take profits or losses depending on which target is hit.

- When you take partial profits or partial losses depending on what the market reveals to you as the trade develops.

Throughout the trading examples, I have shown you how I continually evaluate a trade. When the trade works to your advantage, re-calculate the risk-to-reward ratio with the latest developments and decide whether to take partial profits, whether to re-enter the trade at a better price point, etc.

In the GG trade, when the technical picture became uncertain, the trade was cut short and risk was reduced. The market was indicating that the picture was more uncertain. When it does that, there's no reason to charge full speed ahead despite the uncertainty. Once you begin to realize that there are always so many opportunities in the market, the fixation on any given trade becomes less important. If the risk increases, you should look to reduce that risk – period.

What Would You do Today?

When evaluating your existing trades, the question you should always be asking yourself is *"With respect to this stock, what would I do today?"* This is the simplest way to evaluate whether the trade continues to make sense. If you would be willing to enter the position today, what would the stop loss and profit targets be? What time frame would you trade? How large of a position would you take?

The questions for an existing position are the same questions you would ask yourself for a new position. If you would not take on the trade as a new position, why are you still in the existing one? If the position is not working out as it should, consider a partial exit of the position or a complete liquidation. You should study the chart and formulate a plan to exit at the best possible and realistic price under the current circumstances. The final trade on FXE was exactly this – attempting to find the best possible price point to exit the trade with. The desire is always to maximize your profits and minimize your losses juxtaposed against the risk of doing so. That's always the trade off.

Becoming a Disciplined Trader

An active portfolio manager is a disciplined trader – a trader who engages in risk based future events. Sure there's risk, but it is controlled risk. A disciplined trader is not a trader playing Texas Hold 'Em. A disciplined trader doesn't feel the need to risk everything on the next turn of their playing cards. No, a disciplined trader is a trader who positions themselves appropriately for unknowable future events. They are traders who are constantly managing their positions to reduce risk, carefully using leverage when appropriate, and all the while working the trades to leave the largest amount of money in the best possible trades. A disciplined trader always has their eye on the horizon, searching for gathering storm clouds.

There are certain things you should do and other things that you should avoid as a small trader. When events are scheduled to occur that could significantly help or hurt you, it behooves you to pay attention to those events. Scheduled events are actionable – you can do something about them prior to their happening. Not doing anything about it is not a characteristic of a disciplined trader. The following is a list of commonly scheduled events and how you should approach them:

- Earnings
- Fed Meetings
- Economic Releases

- Organizational Meetings
- Investor Conferences

> **Note:** What action you take heavily depends on how the market approaches the actionable event. In many cases you will see the market *expect* the outcome of an upcoming event to be favorable and thus the market rises in *advance* of the event. When the news arrives and is as expected, *then the market sells off* since the event was already *discounted*. The market usually moves in anticipation of the event. Your job is to judge how the market has positioned prior to the event so you have a better understanding of the reaction once the event occurs.

Earnings

Generally speaking, you should not trade in front of earnings release. Earnings are released four times a year and are usually preceded a couple of weeks by an earnings announcement. You can find earnings dates for the stock you are interested in from a number of free Internet sites.

Occasionally there are earnings pre-announcements and many times they are downside surprises or warnings. These announcements are issued reasonably soon after the earnings quarter is completed. Since earnings are usually announced about three to four weeks after the quarter ends, the risk period is two to four weeks before earnings are announced.

Earnings and earnings pre-announcements can easily move an otherwise moribund stock up or down 5%, 10%, or even 15% in one day. Given the volatility that is associated with earnings and warnings, be especially careful during the announcement period. Always check to see when earnings are due to be released **before** you purchase or short sell a stock. It is typically not in your best interest to step into a stock in front of this scheduled news. If you feel you must, scale down the size of your position to limit the loss if the position moves against you violently.

If you are holding a large position and you do not want to liquidate it in front of earnings, take some measures to reduce your risk. Use options to "buy insurance" against your existing positions. There are many books and web sites available that explain how to do so. View these options as an insurance policy where you end up paying a premium if nothing happens or if something good happens.

A second approach is to lighten up prior to earnings. You don't have to sell your entire position but you can sell some portion of it. One proven method is to remove your principal from the market. If you had 100 shares to begin with and you have a 20% gain in those shares, sell 80% of the shares and keep the remaining 20% of the shares (since these are essentially free). No matter how many shares you remove from the mix, take some money and place it in your pocket leaving less risk for the announcement.

If you find yourself in a losing position going into earnings, sell off some if not all of the shares prior to the earnings announcement. It's a lot better to be safe than sorry.

Fed Meetings

The Federal Reserve is probably the most important single institution in the United States with respect to the equity and currency markets. They have the power to make money easier or harder to obtain through policy decisions and day-to-day open market operations they conduct. All banking institutions must answer to them with respect to their practices, and increasingly there is a larger umbrella of institutions under their control including brokerages.

The Federal Reserve publishes a complete list of their upcoming events and speaking engagements on their Web site (http://www.federalreserve.gov). The chairman of the Federal Reserve, in particular, is in a position to affect the markets. Many times the chairman purposefully does so through speaking engagements and the regularly scheduled Federal Reserve Board meetings where the Federal Funds and Discount Rate changes are announced. In general, it is best not to add positions before the Federal Reserve's policy announcements, but instead wait until the dust has settled afterwards.

Additionally, as the world becomes even more interconnected, the central bank policy decisions of other nations (in particular Europe, Great Britain, and China) also can have significant impact on our domestic markets so it is best that you at least have their rate setting dates on your radar screen as well.

Economic Releases

There are a host of economic releases that occur on a regular schedule – typically either weekly or monthly. These economic data points constantly provide the market with additional information regarding the health of the economy. The health of the economy has a great bearing on the health of the stock market. Some of the more important releases currently include:

- The Department of Labor's weekly first-time unemployment claim filings and the monthly employment report.
- Inflation related data comes out monthly in the CPI and PPI reports.
- Economic activity reports such as the Leading Economic Indicators (LEI), Gross Domestic Product, Personal Income and Spending,

Factory Production and Utilization reports, Durable Goods, etc.
- Sentiment indicators such as the consumer confidence numbers.

All of these indicators are released regularly. Current predictions and actual reported numbers are available through business newspapers and business Internet sites. The importance of an indicator varies over time depending upon what the general economy is doing. There are times, for example, where the employment number is the most important statistic because the prevailing view is that of an impending slowdown in the economy. An increase in the number of people who are unemployed would tend to add confirmation to that theory.

At other times there may be fear that inflation is picking up. If so, the Federal Reserve may have to increase interest rates to battle inflation. In those situations, the PPI and CPI numbers become more critical.

As a trader, you simply need to be aware of what the prevailing mood is, what affect an impending release of scheduled data may have on the markets, and in particular, your positions. If the potential affect is significant, take some steps to reduce your risk prior to the announcements.

Organizational Meetings

On a lesser scale, there are other meetings such as the G7 meeting of Industrialized Nations, the World Bank, and others. They typically have little impact on the equity markets. The G7 is probably the most important since it can have far reaching consequences to the currency markets which in turn move the equity markets. Usually these decisions do not have any immediate affect on the prevailing prices in the market and thus do not typically require immediate action by you.

Investor Conferences

There are many conferences, usually hosted by the larger brokerage firms, that can have reasonably large and immediate share price consequences to individual stocks. If you are trading in individual stocks, it's best to occasionally check out news events on the company's website to see if any presentations are pending. Even if you choose to do nothing in advance of these presentations, being aware of impending news can figure into your trading plan if there is a large positive or negative spike in the price of the company.

Commentary and News

There is a saying that "the release of news is not as important to the market as is the market reaction to the news." How the market reacts depends upon a number of factors that are independent of the actual news. Many times the news provides the excuse for the market to sell off or to rally higher. You should consider that the majority of the news, both political and economic, has characteristics that enable the interpretation to be made in either a bullish or bearish context. As a result, the current market environment ends up shaping the news – not the other way around.

This is the main reason that trading on pending information is so difficult. To be successful you have to both predict the news accurately and the market's reaction to the news accurately! That's difficult!

It's far better to reduce risk before a significant news event rather than to gamble on it. Most of the time there are plenty of trading opportunities that arise once the news has been disseminated and the risk parameters are far more favorable afterwards.

By monitoring what the prevailing view is on upcoming news, then seeing how the market actually reacts to that news, you can formulate these larger picture type thoughts into your thesis formulation and evaluations. Market commentary is offered on a number of sites, most of which are free or have some free portion. Although you don't necessarily want to trade off of commentary, it is good to have a sense for what others who are trading the market are thinking. The following provides a sampling of free sites:

- Forbes (http://www.forbes.com)
- Wall Street Journal (http://online.wsj.com)
- The Financial Times (http://news.ft.com)
- The Economist (http://www.economist.com)
- Smart Money (http://www.smartmoney.com)
- MarketWatch (http://marketwatch.com)
- The Street.com (http://www.thestreet.com)
- TA Today.com (http://www.tatoday.com)

Strong Beliefs are the Most Dangerous

In many ways, the truisms of life are mirrored in the equity markets. For example, some of the most dangerous beliefs are those that are most strongly held. We see in real life that they can result in great grief going so far as to even include war. In the market, if you believe strongly in something and you parlay that belief into a trade, you are much more likely to hold on to that trade even if the market repeatedly informs you that you are wrong. Realize that the more reticent the belief, the more dangerous the trade. If you find yourself fighting the market and taking large losses as a result, step back and consider your beliefs – they are likely to be the root cause for all your financial pain.

Chapter

10

Trade Data - your Trading Diary

M ark Twain once said that "History doesn't repeat itself, but it does rhyme." Your history of trading, both mistakes and successes, will undoubtedly rhyme upon further analysis. If you are comfortable with that history, data analysis is unlikely to be of much benefit. Most of us, however, can greatly benefit from an occasional look back at what we did, why we did it, and the result of those actions.

Tracking Your Trades

It's easy to forget, when you are making your trades, that later analysis of those trades may lead to future changes in the way you trade. In order for your analysis to provide any real benefit, balance how much data you collect with the sheer burden of collecting it. Keeping detailed notes of what you trade can become overwhelming, and the interest in doing so can be lost quickly. As a result, determine the essential data elements needed for effective historical data analysis in the future.

So what are these critical data elements to collect? The majority of the elements to collect are the same ones that you used in creating your risk-to-reward calculations. Here is a recap along with a few newly introduced ones:

- Stock symbol
- Entry date
- Type of trade (long or short sell)
- Number of shares traded
- Entry price
- Stop loss price
- Target price
- Exit date
- Expected duration for the trade
- Technical pattern
- Exit price

From these data points, others can be calculated such as:

- Result of the trade
- Gain or loss percentage
- Actual duration of the trade (in days)

Analyzing the Results

If you keep the data in a spreadsheet, or better yet, a database, you can easily analyze the results over time. Here are some simple questions that can lead to better trading results:

- Of the trades made, what types of trades led to winning trades versus losing ones?
- What were the most profitable trade types?
- What were the trade types that were most likely to succeed?
- What were your total gains versus losses on a weekly, monthly, quarterly, and yearly basis? Is there a pattern where some periods of time are better or worse than others? Why?
- Do most of your gains come from longer term or shorter term trades? Do the majority of your trades deviate from the average number of days where you realized your greatest returns?
- Where did your worst losses occur? Did you violate your entry and/or exit criteria in these trades? In your winning trades, did you follow your entry/exit criteria?
- How well did you estimate the time duration of the trades? Were you mostly over, under, or both? If so, by what percentage? Of those that you were reasonably accurate, were they of a certain type of trade? Is there anything you can

identify with as to why you are more accurate sometimes?

The list of possibilities is seemingly endless. You may even find out later that there are a few more data points that may be worth keeping. For example, I keep tabs on the short, intermediate, and long-term trends in the general market when the trade is placed. I do this to see if there is a correlation between winning and losing trades that go with or against the prevailing trends.

Dwelling on the past is not the issue at hand. Instead, it is important to learn from it. The job of trading is a lonely game. In today's world it is, for the most part, a game of solitaire where individuals from all walks of life stare endlessly at flickering screens while moving piles of money around. If you want to succeed, you have to sharpen your trading tactics and develop an edge that others lack. Analysis of your trading is one way to create that edge. Incorporating what you learn and keeping track of when you do it provides the basis of measuring your performance. It's an endless game of tuning and retuning your trading tactics over time.

Chapter

11

Putting it All Together

The *little guy* has the ability to play a prominent part in the trading history of the 21st century. The trading landscape has changed drastically over the past 30 years and your ability to control your financial future has never been brighter.

Becoming a successful trader is indeed not only possible but probable. You just need to develop a comprehensive understanding of what it takes to be successful, then develop and implement a trading plan that incorporates those ideas. The *little guy* has some distinct advantages over the large trader and most of the disadvantages are no longer significant. The many obstacles of the past no longer litter your development as a successful trader.

What does remain for a small trader to become a successful trader is to spend the time and effort required to acquire the knowledge and tools to trade successfully. To be successful, you first need to commit the time and effort needed to become successful. Once you acquire that mindset, tackle the tasks that make you a successful trader. This includes:

- Developing a practical appreciation for technical analysis (at a minimum do this to sharpen your timing with respect to purchases and sells).
- Start with the big picture and work your way back to the small.
- Create a thesis for what is likely to happen over the next few weeks.
- Pick trades that fit within and complement that thesis.
- Monitor the thesis as time passes and more data points are revealed.
- Keep trading ideas fresh through the use of stock screeners and watch lists.
- Understand and use the trading tools (order types) available to you for trade entry, protection, and exit.
- Actively manage your portfolio. Active portfolio management is probably the single most effective trading skill you can develop. Many times it is the difference between success and failure. Do this by constantly monitoring risk, seeking ways to reduce it, and regularly putting profits into your trading coffers.

- Become a disciplined trader – avoid taking unnecessary and excessive risks.
- Keep track of your trades. Analyze both your successes and failures. Next, incorporate what you learn into what you do going forward.

Above all, enjoy what you do and enjoy the process of learning how to do it better. With a little work, a lot of patience, and a desire to learn and improve, you too can be a successful trader ... the proverbial *little guy*!

Lastly, if time constraints or the lack of desire prevent you from managing your financial future, then think long and hard about whom you employ to do so. Find someone who embraces and employs the crux of the ideas presented here and trades your money as if you are the little guy. TA Today provides such a service and the service is structured such that risks are controlled and charges are dependent upon results. There are likely other services available that embody the same ideas and principles – you just have to seek them out.

Whatever path you choose, enjoy the journey and reap the benefits. Your financial future truly is in your hands, so make the best of it.

INDEX

R

About the Author

Since August of 2007, L.A. Little (a self-taught trader) has worked as a Colorado licensed Investment Advisor Representative managing his own funds as well as those of others. Having treated trading as a full time job since 2001, turning professional was a natural consequence of the path he has chosen.

L.A.'s introduction into the world of trading started in 1989 when he began trading commodities (mostly cotton, sugar and gold). As a computer science graduate, he took to the technical side of trading writing programs to compute stochastic indicators and MACD lines long before they were widely available and common place. From those humble beginnings, his love of trading has taken him to this point – presenting his ideas on how a small trader can profit in the equity markets while controlling risk.

L.A. strongly believes that anyone can learn to trade – that it's more about the desire than some innate knowledge. It is his hope that this book serves to further that learning process for other small traders so that they to can fulfill their financial goals.